DEAR PATRIARCHY

THE GASLIT WOMAN'S GUIDE TO SURVIVING THE (CORPORATE) WORLD

BY JENNIFER AUDRIE AND LISA LYNN

ISBN: 978-1-957723-74-7 (hard cover)
        978-1-957723-75-4 (soft cover)

Edited by: Monika Dziamka

Warren
publishing

Published by WARREN Publishing
Charlotte, NC
www.warrenpublishing.net
Printed in the United States

*This book is dedicated to Clifford Eugene LeBlanc,
the most incredibly insightful and hardworking man who
never ceased to be beautifully amazed by what the women
in his life could achieve. Our most loving, enthusiastic
cheerleader: you are missed every day.*

INTRODUCTION
WHAT MAKES A WOMAN

The experience of being a woman is not a monolith, and we are not representatives for all womankind. The personal stories we share in this book relate to the specific experiences that we have had as cisgender, White women working in the corporate world over the last two decades. Jenni identifies as part of the LGBTQ+ community and is neurodivergent however, there are many lenses of discrimination we do not have personal experience with and cannot personally speak to, because it isn't our place to do so. In those instances, we have included key research and statistical information because it is a necessary and important part of the conversation, but we are not attempting to speak for those who already have a voice. Throughout the book, we have listed educators whose work has opened our eyes and evolved the way in which we see both the workplace and the wider world. We hope they help you as they have helped us.

In the parts of the book which speak about topics that have "traditionally" been considered the realm of women—like menstruation and motherhood—we have endeavored to use language which recognizes that gender expansive people, trans men, and other gender identities may also share, or have shared, these experiences while not identifying as a woman. We have also endeavored to make clear that menstruation, childbirth, and living in a body that was assigned female at birth are not what make you a woman. We believe that gender itself is a societal construct and that society's continued adherence to a binary system of gender is both false and deeply harmful. When we are discussing the different statistics for "men" and "women," we are including all people who identify as a man within the definition of a man, and all people who identify as a woman within that definition. However within a heteropatriarchal context, the statistics are often drawn from the experiences and treatment of cis-het men and women. It is important to recognize that the experiences and treatment of non-binary people, trans men, and trans women in the corporate world are often very different to that of cis-het men and women. What we want to shine a light on in this book are the ways in which a patriarchal society views anything representing as feminine as "less than," which falls under further attack when the lenses of race, disability, and sexual orientation are applied. It should go without saying, but we'll say it here for clarity: trans women are women.

CHAPTER 1
LET'S START AT THE VERY BEGINNING

*I have learned over the years that when one's
mind is made up, this diminishes fear; knowing
what must be done does away with fear.*

–ROSA PARKS

Jenni's Story:

I n August of 2018, I shakily gathered my notes as I headed to the
HR office to report my boss for sexual harassment. I was self-
conscious that I had a skirt and heels on; somehow, I felt like
wearing that would give my story less weight. As I began speaking
to the HR executive, I burst into tears; it was the first time I could
recognize the terrible pressure of what I'd put up with for the last
year. When I initially interviewed for the job, it was with the man I
would eventually report. He was overly familiar from our very first
meeting, and it was very off-putting, like he had decided we were
already best friends even though we'd never met before. My next
interview was, again, with him but in person this time. He arranged
for us to meet at a coffee shop, the informal setting seeming to
underline his uncomfortable assumption of familiarity with me. As
our casual chat became increasingly personal, the unsettling feeling
I had about him turned into outright concern, and I seriously

considered turning down the job when it was offered to me. My husband and I needed me to earn, the job paid well, and it was a great company to work for; surely, I thought, he won't act so familiar in front of other people.

From the moment I started the job, I noticed that there was something covertly sexual in his familiarity: It wasn't full throttle right away; it began with a lot of "playful joking," which then turned into comments on my appearance. I tried to convince myself that they were harmless compliments. It started nonchalantly: "Your hair looks nice today," "I like your outfit," "Those shoes are awesome," etc. As happens in most grooming situations, his sexualization of me grew more overt over time, and things started to get weird. He put a meeting in my calendar called "Professional Development," which turned out to be us meeting at a bar. Again, I was uncomfortable, but this was a new job that I was enjoying, and I saw him being overly familiar with many members of my team, including women I liked and respected. If they were okay with it, why shouldn't I be?

That night he got sloppy drunk, giving me all the details of his open marriage, specifically the "swinging" his wife did that he hadn't done ... yet. As he grew more intoxicated, he told me how great I looked at work, how he loved to flirt, and that I couldn't tell anyone on the team about this because they were like his children. I gritted my teeth and did my best to smile and "play nice," but I woke up the following morning with a sense of dread as I prepared to head into the office. I tried to convince myself I had misunderstood what he had said, forgiving his terrible words as much for my benefit as for his.

When I got to work, he called me into his office and said, "Don't worry; I didn't tell my wife where I was last night."

Now it started to feel dangerous: I wanted to like him because I enjoyed my job and wanted to believe so badly that, somehow, I was mistaken, despite the mounting evidence.

Later that week, in another "one-on-one" meeting, he said, "Hey, we should be dating."

When I reminded him that we were both married, he said, "What if we weren't?"

I tried to laugh it off and left his office as soon as I could, but I knew he'd been offering something and I had rejected it, which worried me. The next day, he stopped talking to me completely, and my work life began to change for the worse. I was put on small, inconsequential projects, well beneath my skill set and pay grade. I worked as hard as I could, but suddenly, the tide had turned, and everything I did and said was wrong. He told some of my colleagues that he didn't appreciate my negative energy and intensity. I took his comments to heart and tried to come across as more positive at work. I put my head down and worked diligently through all the tasks I was given, but it got me nowhere, and I had no support.

Things came to a head a few months later when I was newly pregnant with my third child and he unexpectedly called me into his office for another "one-on-one." He told me he loved pregnant women and made comments about the changes in my face and body.

Horrified, I told him, "You can't talk to me like that," and he got angry.

It was the first time I'd stood up to him directly, the first time I had said no out loud; he didn't like it. Immediately, the conversation turned hurtful, with him saying it had been a huge mistake to hire me, how I had no future at the company, that no one liked me, and I was failing in my role. As he finished his character assassination of me and the meeting came to an end, I knew that this would negatively impact my career. I loved the company I worked for, liked my job, and felt that I was doing good work. Watching him treat the women around me poorly and make inappropriate comments to them as well, I knew I needed to say something. When he wasn't peacocking around the office giving "edgy" compliments to women left and right, he would show people pictures of his wife dressed in costumes and outfits that displayed her breasts and body. It had to stop.

Reporting him to HR took over an hour, and I didn't leave anything out: I had dates, I had details, and I let them have all of it. Following that meeting, I felt guilty for not telling his supervisor first, but when I did manage to get time with her to discuss what I'd done, she didn't take me seriously at first.

Her initial response, when I told her what had happened to make me report him, was, "You're not perfect yourself," to which I replied, "You have someone in a position of power using it inappropriately. That's the problem here," and my statement seemed to sink in. She got in touch with the HR executive, and together they decided that I needed to stay home for a week while they figured out the "next steps."

During that week, he had free rein to tell everyone his version of what had happened, and when I came back to work, I was a pariah. When the situation at work began to spiral out of control, I had looked online for advice on how to get through this kind of situation because I felt alone, unsupported, and like I'd done something wrong. At that time, there was nothing of substance to be found, certainly no first-hand accounts that detailed what I was going through and would warn me that, when I returned to the office, none of my colleagues would speak to me. He, however, greeted me with a huge smile and told me he was glad I was back. I felt sick: I had no protection from him and nothing to help me navigate this hideous situation.

I was stressed and anxious for the entire ten hours of each workday, and not just because of his behavior. I was never given the written report that was laid out as part of the HR reporting process in our employee handbook, and the HR executive told me they had found no "proof" of harassment. Women who had previously told me that they were uncomfortable with his behavior *were now upset with me for mentioning them in confidence to HR. It was made clear to me, every day, that no one was on my side.*

My reporting structure was changed. I was told to report to his boss in the interim, but she wasn't particularly supportive, telling me I would need to recover from the damage the "optics of my actions had caused." She also had no time to direct me, and no one else seemed to know what work I should be doing. The HR executive "checked in" with me at the end of my first week back at work, telling me good luck and that I was to let her know if there was any retaliation. My desk was ten feet from his office, and he would come and stand over me with a huge grin on his face. If we passed in the hallways, he would walk close to me, forcing me against the wall to avoid touching him. In every way he could, he made each workday a torture. It was a daily deluge of stress, anxiety, and fear. I lost my pregnancy to a stillbirth well into the second trimester, and I will always wonder if the constant stress I was under at the time caused me to lose my baby.

I continued to scour the internet to find resources on how to handle reporting sexual harassment, but I found a huge void. There were articles about how a person should legally go about reporting it; there were dry HR documents about how to manage reports of sexual harassment in the workplace; and there were a few Business Insider articles on the "epidemic" of harassing bosses. But there was nothing that really spoke to what I was going through. Nothing told me how to manage my stress levels in the office, or what things I could, and should, demand from the company on my behalf. Nothing I found gave me the information about surviving sexual harassment that I desperately needed. So my sister Lisa and I decided to write an article about it to help those who were, like us, drowning in the corporate world's inherent sexism. That single article idea grew into the idea for a book as we spoke to other working women about how it felt to exist in the corporate world, and so much more came up: systemic racism, ableism, prejudice, queerphobia—the list went on and on. We wanted to give people something to hold onto so they knew they weren't alone, especially when they were having to report colleagues, which is when the gaslighting and manipulation really ramps up. The Patriarchy is loud and proud, and in the past, it has always won because it's such an integral part of our daily lives. It's become as omnipresent, and unnoticed, as our own shadows, and we knew a light needed to be shone on the dark parts of our societies and ourselves that had to change in order to make the world—specifically the corporate world—a more equitable place for all people.

We started writing this book in late 2018 after several attempts to pitch an article about what really happens when you report sexual harassment. There seemed to be no appetite for it even though we really needed to see that content and we knew deep down that other women probably needed it too. We vented to each other about how there was a lack of real-world content to help women navigate the corporate environment—advice that was based on what really happens to women in the workplace, not just gleaned from management books written by men, with men in mind. We needed something focused on the lived experience of women working in a corporate environment that was predominantly built by, and for, men. Something that spoke to the way in which women are asked to twist themselves to fit in, consciously and unconsciously, on a daily basis. Something that prepared us for the negative experiences we might have in the workplace and how we could protect ourselves and others. Coincidentally, this kind of book had been on both of our minds for a few years, and we knew that if we couldn't find it, then other women must also be struggling. If it didn't exist, then we needed to write it ourselves. So here we are, four years, another kid, a cross-country move, and a global pandemic later.

First, let us just say that we want to help because we know it's hard. If we could, we'd build a magical gateway to our, and your, younger selves who bled, sweated, and shed millions of tears battling through some serious adversity. And, before we go any further, one important thing needs to be said: you are not imagining things. The things that seem to be undercutting you, making you feel demeaned or unfulfilled at work, *are* happening. Don't let yourself be gaslit— *trust yourself*. What happens to women in the workforce is often unfair, enraging, and debilitating. We wrote this book because by sharing our mistakes and failures, our triumphs and shortcuts, we're hoping to help ease your burden and get you fired up for success.

We're here for a connection too; we want this book to resonate with you, for you to feel heard and seen, for you to think, "That happened to me!" as you read. For decades, we have felt like we were standing in the background of our careers because the corporate world consistently showed us that it was not okay to be the primary focus. That, somehow, we weren't allowed to be the stars of our professional lives. We watched our male colleagues move up the company ladder by simply showing up while we tried every trick in the book and stagnated. We came to work early and stayed late, worked until midnight and on weekends, went to all the company drinks events and Christmas parties, forced a laugh at inappropriate jokes, and kept our mouths shut about inappropriate behavior, all in an effort to fit in. We tried being the "chameleon" woman who changes herself to suit every different environment that, even today, is often trotted out as the "right way" for a woman to behave in the corporate world. Doing all of these things never yielded any positive results; it only made us unknowable, making it easier to be regarded as faceless cogs in the machine. We were living in a twilight zone where the harder we worked, the less progress we made, and it started to feel like maybe we wanted too much. We began to wonder if we couldn't actually excel in this male-dominated world and that perhaps the most we could hope for was to simply exist.

The writer Casey Gerald once spoke about a sign he saw outside a Stasi work camp that said, "He who adapts can live tolerably,"[1] to which he thought, *Who wants to live tolerably when they can live greatly?* For us, that's a hard agree. We want so much more for you than a tolerable job where the most you can do is just survive the day. We want women to have the work they put in paid back to them in dividends, in whatever form they need it to take. A fair salary based on the actual cost of living, an equitable workplace, to be heard and respected—all of these should be a given, not a one-off. You deserve every single one of these things all of the time, and we want you to have them.

To do this, we need you to come to this book with not just an open mind but an open heart as well, because some of the information we discuss is not easy to read, and some of it may feel really challenging. One of the shortfalls of living in a male-dominated society (which we explain more fully in chapter 3, "The Patriarchy is Not Quiet") is that we as women don't always get the time and space to develop the full experience of what it is to be a woman, which includes the experiences and struggles of women who don't look like or identify the same way as us. That is not to say that we want you to change who you are; twenty or thirty years ago you'd be told that, as a woman, you need to completely change how you present yourself in order to be accepted and elevated within the corporate world.

* * *

We need to pause here and acknowledge that Black women and women of Color, face continual discrimination in both their personal and professional lives simply for the way they look, dress, behave, and speak. This is all part of systemic racism, which we address in more detail in chapter 4, "Looking through Concrete Walls". It plays an integral role in the oppression and erasure of women from these communities within the corporate environment. This is something that White women must take the lead in calling out and actively expelling from the workplace in order for all women to exist and function at the same level. What we are speaking about in this particular section is the drive within the corporate world for women to behave "like men" in order to succeed, but we are not ignoring or glossing over the enormous pressures placed on, specifically, Black women and women of Color within the status quo of the corporate world to "Whiten" themselves in order to succeed.

* * *

Still today, the most prevalent advice for women on how to succeed in the corporate world is to dress, think, talk, and generally act more "like a man" in order to excel. You will not find that here; we know you already have myriad abilities to achieve great things within you, though you may not know how to capitalize on your skill set to your advantage amidst all the obstacles you face in the workplace. In each chapter, we'll share stories of our personal experiences working in the corporate world over the last two decades centered around critical issues that we'll explore through statistics, research, and the knowledge of incredible educators and activists. Our goal is to share information that speaks to your experiences and supports you in the fight to achieve your professional ambitions. At times, making yourself seen and heard in the corporate environment can feel like a battle, and we wish we'd had this kind of resource when we started our careers—when we experienced harassment or bullying, when we were silenced or subordinated, and when we internalized sexism as "the way the world worked." We've made, and continue to make, huge strides in how we view our own presence in the workplace, and we want to break down the obstacles that held us back in case they're holding you back too.

Who are we? We're sisters who spent most of our childhood growing up in a small southern California town that was an uncomfortably close approximation of Pleasantville. When we left school, we tried to see as much of the world as we could afford to, both of us experiencing cultures and countries that we had never learned much about in our predominantly White town and White-centric educational system. We tried to leap into the unknown and explore the world outside of the confines of our childhood, and when it felt like the right time to "settle down," Jenni stayed in the United States (US), while Lisa made a permanent move to the United Kingdom (UK). Somehow, we both stumbled into industries that were not particularly welcoming to women and could be generously described as "male-dominated."

Jenni is a senior project manager in IT and has run multimillion-dollar projects for some of the largest corporations in the country. Just writing this descriptor gave her such bad anxiety (covered in chapter 6, "The Only Woman in the Boardroom"), it made her want to throw out the book and hide. Jenni runs a woman-centric tech consultancy, and she shares three beautiful, high-energy children, aged seven and under, with her husband.

Lisa is a senior project manager for a main contractor in the UK construction industry, helping build landmark London projects for a variety of high-profile clients and focuses on creating and supporting women-lead project teams. Lisa and her partner share a rambunctious five-year-old as well as twin tweens and a towering teen from his previous marriage.

Why are we telling you all this? So you'll know that much of what we discuss in this book hits us hard. We are driven, career-oriented women who want to succeed and have spent our twenties, thirties, and now forties pursuing excellence. We are also mothers to a shit ton of kids, all of whom need us in different ways, all of the time.

* * *

We need to quickly hit pause again to say to the childless people who read this book that, although we do speak about having children in this book, we recognize that having children is not the default status for someone who identifies as a woman. You do not need to have children to be a fully realized woman, nor does not having children make balancing your work life and personal life any easier. We speak in chapter 5, "You Can't Have It All," about what it means to "have it all," and that term includes having children only because that is the societal expectation of women. Women who do not have children are deemed "selfish" or "unfeminine," which we absolutely don't agree with. Perhaps when you read parts of the book like chapter 8, "The Penalty for Leaning Out," where we discuss the motherhood paradox and penalty, you'll gain new insight into the struggles mothers who also work outside the home face. However, if you read it and feel it's not relevant to you, or you feel bombarded by the discussion, we fully understand if you want to skip a page or two.

* * *

We continually struggle to keep all the plates spinning, much less aloft, and the number of times we have hysterically cried on the phone to each other because we just cannot make our lives work like they're "supposed to" is beyond measure. We've spent so much time trying to figure out why intelligent, driven, capable women like us can't make the concept of "having it all" actually work. We kept getting caught up in the trope that women *could* have it all, as long as they were willing to work for it incessantly (and never fail). It took us a few years to realize that we weren't failing; it just wasn't physically or emotionally possible to keep a fulfilling and evolving career in balance with a personal life that, for us, included children and a partner. Everyone and everything seemed to need our constant support or attention, and there simply wasn't enough of us to go around. Our personal needs and self-care were the first to get put on hold, and from that point onwards (and also because of it), we began to lose ourselves, which was swiftly followed by the loss of a happy home life and productive professional progression. The harder we tried to have it all, the more we lost the pieces of ourselves that we desperately needed. So, with the constant simmer of resentment climbing up our walls, we finally allowed ourselves to see what we'd been ignoring for so long: there's a serious problem here.

Admittedly, the problem had always been there—the constant pressure on us to be the right kind of woman for every situation— even though it never allowed us to be ourselves and we never felt entirely accepted. We struggled for years to force ourselves into the corset of what it meant to be a woman, an ambitious earner, a mother who also chooses to work outside the home. The strain of trying to keep everything balanced was killing us. It was starving us of joy, strangling us in the boardroom, and driving a wedge between us and our loved ones. Our heads and hearts were totally disconnected. If you asked us how we felt, we couldn't find the words to tell you what we needed or wanted. All we knew was that the one constant, the daily feeling we woke up to and fell asleep with, was that we were somehow wrong. There always seemed to be something wrong with our version of womanhood: too opinionated, too loud, too smart, too weird, too ambitious, wanting too much for our lives. We couldn't force ourselves to stay at companies where we were constantly undervalued, patronized, and harassed.

Each time one of us would start a new job, we'd say, "They really seem to get me here; my boss is nice but not in a pervy way. The men seem friendly, but like 'normal' friendly, not 'creepy' friendly, and I could see a lot of women around the office, so I think this one might work out long-term."

We'd start, and then, of course, the cracks would begin to show. First, we'd find out that most of the women we saw in the office worked in low-paying jobs and were routinely harassed or demeaned by male staff members. At a team drinks event, one of our male colleagues would tell us how great we looked as he slid closer to us along the bar, his hand trying to lift the hem of our dress. Anyone we mentioned it to would tell us that he was "always like that when he drank" and to just avoid him, not to report him as it "wasn't worth it."

Then, a few weeks later, a director would walk into the breakroom while we were bending down to get something out of the fridge and say, "I recognize that bum," in his friendliest tone like he had solved a riddle instead of behaving inappropriately.

We'd get told in a work review that we needed to focus on talking less and listening more, a critique that was never raised to our equally verbose male colleagues. A new director would join the team and make dissecting our work his daily task, raising concerns about us to board members to skew their view of our ability, only for our work to eventually be used, but with his name on it, not ours. Finally, the day would come when we would be openly propositioned by our line manager, who would heatedly suggest that all of our conversations up until now had been leading up to it.

"Don't pretend you don't feel it too," he'd say.

So it would be back out to the market to find a company where there would be less male influence and more powerful women, more freedom to expand, more space to be the efficient, high-functioning leaders that we knew we could be. Yet each time we sat down in an interview and had to explain why we had left our last company, we (the victims) had to gloss over the creative theft, the sexualization, the wasting of our precious time so that we didn't get stuck with the label of "bitter" or "difficult" in the small ponds of our specific industries. We still have yet to find our "forever homes" in the corporate world, and maybe we never will. Perhaps we are puzzle pieces that evolve over time, and we just don't fit in the same situation forever. Maybe you're like that too.

There was another problem going on as well. Everywhere we looked, we could see pervasive, systemic discrimination, which magnified itself in the workplace. We saw (and continue to see) the continual attack of explicit racism on Black people and people of Color everywhere we looked. We saw fatphobia; we saw prejudice; we saw ableism and an overriding queerphobia insidiously flourishing. When all of these discriminatory practices coalesced, they created work environments where people were afraid to be themselves, to show their beautiful uniqueness, where diversity wasn't welcome even though research has shown for years that it significantly improves a company's financial and creative performance.

The importance of unlearning discriminatory conditioning isn't usually raised as a key point when discussing how to propel women toward excellence in the workplace; but it should be. Besides upholding seriously dangerous and damaging social inequity, internalized discrimination is a terminal blockage on the path to authentic creativity and success. Put simply: you can't be the most effective version of yourself if your emotional and cultural intelligence is impaired. We need you to do the work, as we are doing, to find the stories of people who don't look like you, whose voices you haven't heard before, and listen to their truth so that it can become part of your world experience. For White people in particular, there is work to be done in accepting our role in oppression, no matter how unconscious some might feel it to be. Just know that within our current social construct, it is unavoidable—all of us are taught to be racist, misogynist, ableist, and prejudiced. It takes strength to recognize it within ourselves and to start to heal from its damaging impact. We talk more about this in chapter 4, "Looking through Concrete Walls," as well as highlight some excellent teachers who can aid you on the path to unlearning internalized racism specifically.

We want this book to be as inclusive as possible, but we know that we will fall short because of our inherent limitations in being cisgender, White women. We will make mistakes within these pages; we can only draw from research about the impact of racism, prejudice, ableism, fatphobia, and queerphobia in the corporate workspace. We cannot fully capture the pain and frustration of the experiences of Black women and women of Color within the White-centric corporate world, but we will continue to educate ourselves and share the work of the women (and men) we are learning from in order to become better success partners (more on that also in chapter 4, "Looking through Concrete Walls"). We welcome all women to these pages as our sisters, and we apologize for showing up late and without the understanding and action that has long been deserved from us. We hope to be the allies, accomplices, and success partners that have been missing for far too long.

Everything we cover within the pages of this book are things that we passionately believe are holding women back from achieving true and fulfilling professional success. We wanted to bring as much knowledge, research, and history into this conversation as we could, but we fully acknowledge that there is much more information out there to delve into. If you feel, as you read this book, that there is more to add, we invite you to share it with us. We would love to hear your experience of what we have put together; if it has brought you knowledge and, therefore, power that you didn't have before, or if it has side-lined your experience in the workplace, we definitely need to hear from you. Again, we know that we will not get it 100 percent right, but we are trying to be better, do better, and help others. We invite you to join us on the journey and help change the way women are seen and valued within the predominantly cis-het, non-disabled, White male structure of the corporate environment.

So, with all that said, welcome to the gaslit woman's guide to working in the corporate world. Let's go blow the fucking doors off.

CHAPTER 2
WE DON'T HATE MEN

*A feminist is anyone who recognizes the equality
and full humanity of women and men.*
–GLORIA STEINEM

For the record, we don't hate men. We love men, on an individual basis, for the innumerable traits that make you love a person: intelligence, kindness, humor, generosity, etc. If you're a man reading this book, your presence is welcome and appreciated here. We want you to be involved in this exploration of women's experiences in the corporate world. We know that it won't be an easy book to read as it targets the behavior of cis-het men, both in the corporate world and in society who, you may feel, are being unfairly targeted at the moment. Let us first say that, yes, we know #notallmen say the things or exhibit the behaviors that we describe in this book. Not all men actively work to invalidate the existence, skills, and achievements of women, Black people and people of Color, members of the LGBTQ+ communities, marginalized religions, or those with disabilities. Not all men speak over women in meetings, and not all men loudly denigrate their colleagues as "gay" for wearing a pink shirt or showing emotion. Not all men rate the women in their office on "tit size" or openly debate who would be better in bed. Not all men create and participate in a company culture that encourages the sharing of racist material, the objectification of women, or the alienation of work colleagues who don't fit the mold of what is currently accepted as "normal."

We hope that you don't do those things, but a lot of your friends and colleagues absolutely do; maybe someone you manage or that manages you does it. Enough research has shown that the experiences discussed in this book are not just happening; they are happening prolifically. The rise of movements like MeToo, Black Lives Matter, Time's Up, and Everyone's Invited have focused our gaze on why the excuse of "boys being boys" is unacceptable for misogynist, racist, ableist, fatphobic, queerphobic, or otherwise discriminatory behavior. And not just because it's dangerous to the victims, but because its perpetrators are in danger as well. Discriminatory behaviors strengthen and extend the pervasive reach of the patriarchal institutions and discriminatory stereotypes that smother people with expectations and roles that they can't achieve and can't escape. They force men into presenting as strong, unemotional, and utterly self-reliant, which prevents them from asking for help as it's considered a sign of weakness. It's why some men have difficulty forming intimate, meaningful relationships, leaving them prone to developing depression and other mental health disorders. It's also why depression is particularly hard to identify in men as many confuse symptoms of depression with feeling stressed or angry, leading them to act out aggressively or anesthetize themselves through substance abuse. All of this falls under "toxic masculinity" (which we discuss further in chapter 3, "The Patriarchy Is Not Quiet"), and it is the reason why in the UK, 75 percent of all suicides are committed by men[2] and why, globally, men commit suicide at twice the rate of women.[3]

Patriarchal conditioning can leave men unprepared to be supportive friends, partners, and fathers. Many men struggle with allowing their sons to cry and vent their emotions naturally, or letting their boys be babied and coddled in the same way most young girls are. It can be hard to release internalized programming around boys needing to be tough and that the only way for a boy to play "properly" is getting dirty and scraped up. If you have a boy who loves to be covered in mud and bleeding from his knees and elbows, then so be it, but it's not the only way boys play. Some boys like to have painted nails, dress up as fairies, or carry around a purse—and this is just as normal as girls loving dinosaurs, monster trucks, and getting dirty while they play. These behaviors don't need to mean anything about your child's gender identity, and forcing traditional gender roles on young children by fixating on the "right way" for them to play is how toxic masculinity seeps into the experience of childhood and can profoundly damage children. For a man, the pull of the Patriarchy can be very strong when you're raising children, and the only way to resist its insidious effect is to root it out from within yourself. We invite men in particular to "do the work" by learning to recognize how the Patriarchy manifests in you and reprogramming the way you see yourself and the world around you so that if you decide to raise children of your own, the patriarchal chain will finally be broken.

This work is essential, whether or not you have children, for yourself and your adult relationships. It will enable you to have conversations with the people in your life who are still caught in toxic masculinity, misogyny, and other systems of control that fall under the umbrella of the Patriarchy. As our favorite therapist likes to say, the work doesn't stop with you; all you can do is put the work in every day. You may not be able to turn the tide of the Patriarchy in your lifetime, but you can certainly slow the flow of it and make change easier for those who come after you.

If you think that this sounds a bit extreme, that you don't recognize any of the above in yourself, that it's other men who need to do this work, bear with us a bit longer. In 1988, a senior research scientist named Peggy McIntosh wrote an essay detailing her exploration of male privilege and her own White privilege. Within that essay, she outlined a White privilege checklist that is a deep dive into her own privilege in a society dominated not only by men but also by "Whiteness" (McIntosh's original checklist is included in chapter 4, "Looking through Concrete Walls").[4] In 2001, political cartoonist and commentator Barry Deutsch adapted McIntosh's White privilege checklist to detail his own male privilege and published it. Prefacing his checklist, Deutsch wrote the following:

> *Pointing out that men are privileged in no way denies that sometimes bad things happen to men. In the end, however, it is men and not women who make the most money; men and not women who dominate the government and the corporate boards; men and not women who dominate virtually all of the most powerful positions of society. And it is women and not men who suffer the most from intimate violence and rape; who are the most likely to be poor; who are, on the whole, given the short end of patriarchy's stick. As Marilyn Frye has argued, while men are harmed by patriarchy, women are oppressed by it.*[5]

We invite you to read through his checklist and ask yourself honestly how much of what you have achieved in your life and career would have been possible if the obstacles detailed below *had* impacted upon you. Think of privilege as less about opportunities you were given and more about the challenges you didn't have to face.

The Male Privilege Checklist[6]

1. My odds of being hired for a job when competing against female applicants are probably skewed in my favor. The more prestigious the job, the larger the odds are skewed.
2. I can be confident that my coworkers won't think I got my job because of my sex—even though that might be true.
3. If I am never promoted, it's not because of my sex.
4. If I fail in my job or career, I can feel sure this won't be seen as a black mark against my entire sex's capabilities.
5. I am far less likely to face sexual harassment at work than my female coworkers are.
6. If I do the same task as a woman, and if the measurement is at all subjective, chances are people will think I did a better job.
7. If I'm a teen or adult, and if I can stay out of prison, my odds of being raped are so low as to be negligible.
8. I am not taught to fear walking alone after dark in average public spaces.
9. If I choose not to have children, my masculinity will not be called into question.
10. If I have children but do not provide primary care for them, my masculinity will not be called into question.
11. If I have children and provide primary care for them, I'll be praised for extraordinary parenting if I'm even marginally competent.
12. If I have children and pursue a career, no one will think I'm selfish for not staying at home.
13. If I seek political office, my relationship with my children, or who I hire to take care of them, will probably not be scrutinized by the press.

14. Chances are, my elected representatives are mostly people of my own sex. The more prestigious and influential the elected position, the more likely this is to be true.
15. I can be somewhat sure that if I ask to see "the person in charge," I will face a person of my own sex. The higher up in the organization the person is, the surer I can be.
16. Chances are that, as a child, I was encouraged to be more active and outgoing than my sisters.
17. As a child, I could choose from an almost infinite variety of children's media featuring positive, active, non-stereotyped heroes of my own sex. I never had to look for it; male protagonists were (and are) the default.
18. Chances are that, as a child, I got more teacher attention than girls who raised their hands just as often.
19. If my day, week, or year is going badly, I need not ask of each damaging episode or situation whether or not it has sexist overtones.
20. I can turn on the television or glance at the front page of the newspaper and see people of my own sex widely represented every day, without exception.
21. If I'm careless with my financial affairs, it won't be attributed to my sex.
22. If I'm careless with my driving, it won't be attributed to my sex.
23. I can speak in public to a large group without putting my sex on trial.
24. If I have sex with many people, it won't make me an object of contempt or derision.
25. There are value-neutral clothing choices available to me; I can choose clothing that doesn't send any particular message to the world.
26. My wardrobe and grooming are relatively cheap and consume little time.

27. If I buy a new car, chances are I'll be offered a better price than a woman buying the same car.

28. If I'm not conventionally attractive, the disadvantages are relatively small and easy to ignore.

29. I can be loud with no fear of being called a shrew. I can be aggressive with no fear of being called a bitch.

30. I can ask for legal protection from violence that happens mostly to men without being seen as a selfish special interest since that kind of violence is called "crime" and is a general social concern. (Violence that happens mostly to women is usually called "domestic violence" or "acquaintance rape" and is seen as a special interest issue.)

31. I can be confident that the ordinary language of day-to-day existence will always include my sex (for example: "All men are created equal," "mailman," "chairman," "freshman," "he").

32. My ability to make crucial decisions and my capability, in general, will never be questioned depending on what time of the month it is.

33. I will never be expected to change my name upon marriage or questioned if I don't change my name.

34. The decision to hire me will never be based on assumptions about whether or not I might choose to have a family sometime soon.

35. Every major religion in the world is led primarily by people of my own sex. Even God, in most major religions, is usually pictured as being male.

36. Most major religions argue that I should be the head of my household, while my wife and children should be subservient to me.

37. If I have a wife or live-in girlfriend, chances are we'll divide up household chores so that she does most of the labor, particularly the most repetitive and unrewarding tasks.
38. If I have children with a wife or girlfriend, chances are she'll do most of the childrearing, particularly the dirtiest, repetitive, and most unrewarding parts of childrearing.
39. If I have children with a wife or girlfriend, and it turns out that one of us needs to make career sacrifices to raise the kids, chances are we'll both assume the career sacrificed should be hers.
40. Magazines, billboards, television, movies, pornography, and virtually all media is filled with images of scantily-clad women intended to appeal to me sexually. Such images of men exist but are much rarer.
41. On average, I am under less pressure to be thin than my female counterparts are. If I am fat, I probably suffer fewer social and economic consequences for being fat than fat women do.
42. If I am heterosexual, it's improbable that I'll ever be beaten up by a spouse or lover.
43. Complete strangers generally do not walk up to me on the street and tell me to "smile."
44. On average, I am not interrupted by women as often as women are interrupted by men.
45. I have the privilege of being unaware of my male privilege.

While not every circumstance described above will resonate with you, many of them will, no doubt, leave you with questions about how differently society treats men and women. We're asking you to hang on to that feeling and use it as you experience the world. When you see how women are spoken to, talked about, and treated in the corporate environment as well as the wider world, ask yourself: Is this right? Is this fair? Challenge yourself to question what you see happening every day because misogyny, racism, and discrimination are built into even the most minute details of life. All we're asking is that you don't turn away from these questions or dismiss them as being "how the world works" because no matter your age, you'll have lived through at least one cultural shift that has changed "how the world works." Being on the right side matters, being a good man matters, and to look at it more topically, there is nothing more attractive than a man who can freely give and receive love to those around him and show respect to all women whether or not he identifies the same way as them, agrees with them, or likes them. That's a fact.

Another fact is that women in the workplace are struggling, and they need your support. Here's a non-exhaustive list of how you can show your support:

How to not be "that guy":

1. Don't explain anything to a woman unless you have specifically been asked for an explanation.
2. Don't interrupt a woman while she's speaking.
3. If another man interrupts a woman who is speaking, stop him and bring the conversation back to the woman who was interrupted.
4. Don't tell, or laugh at, rape jokes or jokes that objectify, demean, or sexualize women.
5. Don't use misogynistic language like calling women "bitches," refer to anything in a derogatory way as being "like a girl" or feminine, refer to women talking as a "mother's meeting" or "gossips," or designate a woman as "team mom."
6. If you manage women, regularly check in with them to understand how they are experiencing their work

environment. Believe women when they say they feel uncomfortable or are being treated poorly.

7. If you take action/report someone on behalf of a woman, regularly check in and make sure there's been no retaliation on them. Again, believe women if they say retaliation is taking place.

8. Don't steal women's ideas and use them as your own.

One final important fact is that working mothers have it hard, especially when they also choose to work outside of the home. Motherhood itself effectively works out to 2.5 jobs each day, according to a study done by Welch's, with a workday that starts at 6:23 and ends at 20:31, seven days a week, amounting to a ninety-eight-hour workweek.[7] So we really need you, and your friends, to change your language when it comes to talking about mothers. We also need the kind of partnership you give to working mothers to change as well.

Based on our experiences and what we've heard from other working mothers, here's how you (and your friends) can help working mothers.

How to Show Up for Your Partner (& Working Moms Everywhere):

1. **Acknowledge that all mothers work, whether or not they get paid for it.** Remembering to get more toothpaste, stocking the fridge, booking doctor appointments, remembering clothes and shoe sizes, buying Christmas presents, checking in on family members, cleaning the house, washing dishes, cooking, managing the family social calendar—it's all work that you probably don't do, but it needs to be done, so women tend to do it, and they get no pay (and often, no thanks) for it. If you say

that mothers "don't work," it means you don't believe that what women do to keep a household and a family running has any merit, and that's deeply disrespectful. Stop saying it.

2. **Take all of your allocated parental leave and actively engage with your child(ren) and partner.** In the US 60 percent of eligible men take paternity leave,[8] while only 31 percent of eligible men take paternity leave in the UK.[9] To the nonparticipating 40 percent of American men and the 69 percent of British men, we have two questions: why would you not want to spend time getting to know your new baby, and why do you not want to help your partners survive what can be the most painful, exhausting, and life-changing experience of their lives? Many new fathers complain that they feel pushed out or unnecessary. We are speaking from experience when we say you need to push yourself right back in, and the best way to start is by taking all of your parental leave. You don't magically become a mother when you give birth. It's a learning process. If you don't insert yourself into the learning process, you will get left behind. If you're using the line of not being "nurturing" enough, you need to know that a large part of toxic masculinity is the denial of boys' and men's ability to nurture, which is bullshit. Boys can be very nurturing, but they usually need to be taught how and encouraged to do it, just like girls are. An important note to end on is that multiple studies have shown that children perform exponentially better at school and tend to have more successful outcomes in life when they have an active father figure in their lives. Be the father figure that your children need and don't leave your partner drowning in parenthood alone.

3. **Protect your time with your family, despite the potential career penalty.** Go to every school play, sports day, and competition that you can. We know that your career is essential and that it may well support your entire household, but one of the main reasons why women get sidelined in the corporate world is that they don't usually have a choice in showing up for their children. They need to be there because their partners can't be, and when they do this, they get penalized for their lack of commitment to work. Now imagine if it wasn't just working mothers who made this commitment to their family but working fathers too. Would single men and women lead every corporation? Clearly not. The corporate world would have to shift to accommodate this behavior, but it's not shifting right now because it's disproportionately women who protect their time with their children. By actively engaging in the protection of family time within the workplace, you're helping shift both the cultural norm and corporate expectations—a double whammy.

4. **Know (and show) that your partner's career is just as important as yours.** This means you value your partner's career through thick and thin, in the bad times when it interferes with your work responsibilities, not just on payday. Mothers who also work outside the home already struggle to balance the demands of their families and their employers, so don't be another roadblock on the path to success. Ask what support your partner specifically needs, take on responsibilities that you can see aren't being dealt with, and actively engage with what is going on in your family and your home so you can see, without having to ask, where extra help is needed. And please, for the love of God, put your dirty clothes in the laundry basket, not next to it.

5. **Raise *all* of your children to be smart and strong.** When you raise girls as well as boys to be smart and strong, you're modeling what respect looks like. And always remember that the way your girls see you interact with other women is a model for how they expect to be treated by men, especially when you get angry, a time when discriminatory conditioning tends to surface. Being a father is a huge responsibility, not least because you're essentially creating the prototype for how your boys and girls will interact, as adults, with other men. If that seems heavy, it is. Why do you think "daddy issues" is such a popular insult to sling at women who struggle with intimacy? But who do you think is really at fault here—the little girl or the father who didn't show up in a healthy, consistent way?

6. **Raise all of your children to be comfortable expressing emotion and vulnerability.** This means letting boys cry, showing them it's okay to be vulnerable by modeling it yourself, teaching them that being a man is not about empty machismo, winning at all costs, being in control, and using violence as an emotional outlet. Show them that being gentle and kind and expressing love is what really makes a man. If you struggle with this yourself, then you have important work to do. If you don't do the work, you'll be building the same cage for your children that was built for—and still encases—you. If you want to make a start on this journey, we recommend the work of Jackson Katz and the Better Man Movement as a starting point.

7. **Create a genuine partnership where work and family demands are balanced.** Creating a true partnership takes all of the above and incorporates it into the relationships you already have with your partner and children. While the first and most important relationship you have is with yourself,

the second most important is the one you have with your partner. How are you loving each other every day? How are you showing up for each other? Speaking as mothers ourselves, we know that sometimes the most explicit love language you can use is when you make space for us to rest. When you tell us you've got it, and you actually do have it, we can let go of the reins and refill ourselves emotionally/spiritually/physically and come back to you and to the family as our best selves. Speak to your partner and find out how they need you to love and support them and do that, regardless of how your friends, family, or work colleagues view it. It's your balance, not theirs.

8. Show up every day for your partnership. That's it. That's the whole thing.

At the end of all this, it's important to say that men, particularly White men, are ideally placed for enacting the change we need to make the corporate playing field, and the wider world, equitable. Your voices are loud because you disproportionately hold positions of power around the world so please make the choice to use it every day in order to uplift those around you who are being steamrolled by the White-centric, male-centric, non-disabled, cis-het, status quo. Maybe you are helping to enact change in your own company or industry right now. If you are, thank you, and we love you even more than we did before.

To learn more, please check out these additional resources:

Books / Resources

- BetterMan Conference (www.bettermanconference.com)
- Ford, Clementine. *Boys Will Be Boys: Power, Patriarchy and Toxic Masculinity*. London: Oneworld Publications, 2020.

- Katz, Jackson. *The Macho Paradox: Why Some Men Hurt Women and How All Men Can Help (How to End Domestic Violence, Mental and Emotional Abuse, and Sexual Harassment)*. Naperville, Illinois: Sourcebooks, 2019.
- Manne, Kate. *Entitled: How Male Privilege Hurts Women*. New York: Crown, 2021.
- Promundo (www.promundoglobal.org)
- Rosenkranz, Mark. *White Male Privilege*. Small Little Red Press, 2018.

Activists/ Influencers

- ALOK *they/them*
  - Instagram @alokvmenon
  - Facebook @AlokVMenon
- comradekam *he/they*
  - Instagram @itscomradekam
  - TikTok @comradekam
- radicalwholeness A•Key•Lah
  - Instagram @a.key.lah
  - TikTok @radicalwholeness
- Richie Reseda *he/him*
  - Instagram @richiereseda
- Schuyler Bailar *he/him*
  - Instagram @pinkmantaray
  - Facebook @pinkmantaray
  - Tiktok @pinkmantaray

CHAPTER 3
THE PATRIARCHY IS NOT QUIET

I myself have never been able to find out precisely what
feminism is: I only know that people call me a feminist whenever
I express sentiments that differentiate me from a doormat.
–REBECCA WEST

Lisa's Story:

I sat in a boardroom, the only woman in a group of fifteen men around a long oval table. I was twenty-eight at the time, easily ten years younger than the youngest man in the room. A few of the men knew me, but most were unaware of who I was, what I did, and why I was there. And it showed. As the meeting, the "kick off" for a new build project, started, the lead for the client asked us all to introduce ourselves and then started to run through the agenda items. As he went through the list, I became increasingly aware that my voice wasn't exactly welcome. Besides being cut off or talked over while I was speaking, one man in particular clearly didn't warm to me and refused to speak directly to me, either in response to my questions or in asking questions of me. As the lead project manager for the main contractor managing the build works, my presence at the table was an integral part of the conversation—but this man insisted on directing all his questions *and answers intended for me to the man on my left. Luckily for me, this person was a subcontractor of mine that I had asked to attend in order to answer detail-oriented questions about a specific installation for the project. This conversation by proxy threw him off balance, not least because he couldn't answer the questions being asked of him, only I could, so the bizarre three-way in which he had to redirect communication to and from me continued on. He, and several others around the table, were clearly bewildered by this man's refusal to speak directly to me, but they didn't stop it from happening or even comment on it. After a painful hour of this awkward verbal ping-pong, the meeting came to an end, and everyone stood to leave. My subcontractor stayed behind to privately ask if I was okay and said that he'd never seen anything like that before in a professional setting. I told him that I was used to misogynistic behavior as I was typically the only woman in these meetings and that working in a male-dominated industry like construction wasn't easy. To my amazement, he told me I needed to be careful, that making it a gender issue would make people think I had a chip on my shoulder and I'd never "get ahead." I hold qualifications equal to, or in excess of, the qualifications held by any man in the room that day, so I was (and still am) at a loss as to what I should have attributed that bizarre behavior to, if not gender discrimination. I should mention that this took place in 2011, just a decade ago. Behaviors have improved a bit since that time, but as only 15 percent of the UK construction industry employees are women[10] and 72 percent of those women have had to report some kind of discrimination,[11] I think it's safe to say that this stronghold of masculinity hasn't changed much since all those men around the table silently agreed that my voice and presence weren't worth recognizing or fighting for.*

In the US, there are more male CEOs named John than there are female CEOs[12] and, globally, women account for less than 7 percent of national leaders and 2 percent of presidents.[13] There has never been a female pope, nor are women allowed to be members of the Catholic clergy (i.e., bishops, priests, or deacons).[14] There has never been a female American president or secretary-general of the United Nations (UN), and a woman has never been governor of the Bank of England.[15] In 2022, there are thirty-one economies where a women can't obtain a passport in the same way as a man, and in thirty-four economies, a woman can't choose where to live in the same way as a man. There are also restrictions on the types of jobs a woman can hold around the world. In Argentina, women can't polish glass; in Belarus, they can't drive buses carrying more than fourteen people; in China, they can't work in mines;[16] and in Russia, where women make 30 percent less than men on average, there are ninety-eight different jobs that a woman is barred from holding.[17] If we look to the past, women make up only .5 percent of recorded history, a span of roughly five thousand years, despite having always made up approximately 50 percent of the population.[18] Why? Why are women routinely subjugated and relegated to secondary positions within society? Why have women's voices, experiences, and narratives been overwhelmingly silenced and edited out of our collective social history for nearly five millennia? And why, in the twenty-first century, are women still being disproportionately sidelined and penalized in both the wider world and the workplace? Are you sitting in meeting where you get talked over, infantilized, belittled, or harassed?

While fundamental questions like these never have a single reason behind them, the central answer is a phrase you may have heard before but might not have fully understood: the Patriarchy. Allow us to blow your mind.

****

Bear with us as we do a deep dive on this topic. In order to truly understand what the Patriarchy is, its omnipresence, and how it's impacting you on every level, we need to go right back to its roots.

****

The Patriarchy is a social construct where men predominantly hold power in political leadership, religious institutions, economic systems, social privilege, and control of property. A patriarchal society controls you in every way imaginable, from your career options to the clothes you're "allowed" to wear, the way in which society views you, the company you keep, and the things you say. Dominion over women and people who can give birth is crucial within a patriarchal society because, at its simplest level, the only way to know who the "Patriarch" (Father) is, is by controlling access to the person who made him one. Patriarchal societies are based on command and control—our identities and, therefore, our lives are separated into distinct groupings. People are separated by their gender, race, nationality, sexual orientation, and religious beliefs in order for control to be more easily wielded over them. When you start to understand what the Patriarchy looks like, you'll begin to see it everywhere, even in the subtle nuances of daily minutiae like "Mr." being the default title on every internet drop-down box and why women must choose between "Miss," "Ms," and "Mrs" because they are defined by their relationship status and men are not.[19]

Some of this might be hard to believe, and, yes, we know it sounds like we're describing an evil "Big Brother" who runs the entire world, but it's not just one person perpetuating the Patriarchy: it's all of us. You have been force-fed patriarchal logic and control since you were a child, especially as a little girl when you were taught to be quiet and demure, to not make a mess, to always be kind, happy, and of service to others. And what do we teach boys?

We let them "run it out," we give them sturdier toys, and when even these toys get broken, we roll our eyes and say "boys will be boys." We hold boys to minimal standards of responsibility well into their twenties, while we force girls into early maturity by policing their "distracting" bodies before they're even teenagers. We demand that girls (and women) be as small and quiet as possible because that's the way society finds us palatable and appealing. Where did this dichotomous treatment of children, based solely on their assigned sex, come from, and when did it start?

Unsurprisingly, a pervasive social construct like this doesn't just appear overnight, and there are many theories about how it started. Surviving figurines from the period of time starting at 40,000 BCE (a time known as the Upper Palaeolithic period when art first started to appear) right up to 5000 BCE, when humans started recording history, depicted women 90 percent of the time. Women had property rights and owned land. They wrote poetry and held esteemed status in society as high priestesses, queens, and elders. So what happened? Incredibly, there is no central theory that is universally touted; some research points to the rise of plough agriculture which required increased upper-body strength and therefore rewarded and centralized those who tended to have more of it (i.e. men);[20] other research theorized that the rise of tribal militarization shifted the balance of power between men and women.[21]

Dr. Gerda Lerner, a pioneer in advancing women's history as a valid academic field in the 1960s, believes the imbalance developed very gradually from around 3100 BCE in response to the nurturing responsibilities women naturally took on so that children could be born and nursed. This new social organization, created by men and women together, gave rise to a sexual division of labor that allowed a tribe to survive in a time when women's average lifespan was around twenty-eight years, and the infant mortality rate was approximately 75 percent. This sexual division of work was combined with the practice of women agreeing to marry into other tribes to form alliances and protect their own tribes. These customs formed the basis of the belief that men possessed rights that women did not.[22]

When militant tribalism began to develop around 3100 BCE, women and children were taken as prisoners while male prisoners were killed. The capturing of women and children marked the development of class distinctions as enslaved women and children were viewed as property, which gave rise to the idea for, and practice of, the enslavement of people.[23] The coordinated exploitation of women's sexuality and reproductive powers also stems from this time and is, as we've said, a pillar of patriarchal oppression.

Because history has, until recently, been predominantly recorded by men, women's roles in the development of the world as we know it have been downplayed or ignored, which is why we find traditional history books are heavy on the mention and praise of men yet very light on the achievements of women. We learn about Julius Caesar, Alexander the Great, Tutankhamen, and Genghis Khan, but very few of us were taught about the badass queens and warriors of the past like Queen Amanirenas who ruled Kush (an ancient kingdom in modern-day Sudan) from 40–10 BCE, fought the Roman Empire from 27–22 BCE and won. People living outside of Vietnam weren't taught about Trung Trac and Trung Nhi, sisters from the first century CE, who led a rebellion against the Chinese Han dynasty in 39 CE and rode elephants into battle with 80,000 Vietnamese soldiers, including thirty-six female generals. The same is true of Queen Zenobia of Palmyra (a Roman province in modern-day Syria), who ruled from 267 CE, revolted against Roman rule, and conquered Egypt and a vast swath of Asia Minor. If you're like us, you only ever learned about the Roman Empire from a purely (White) male perspective. Don't you wish you'd learned about these incredible women when you were in school? Would you still have wanted to be a zombie cheerleader for Halloween?

The women many of us learn about in history class are Helen of Troy, Cleopatra, Boudicca, Anne Boleyn, and Joan of Arc. Why do these specific women survive in our shared history? Because their stories were either titillating or could be used as an example of what happens to those who step outside of the accepted "gender norms" of their time. History tends to retain women whose stories are either highly sexualized or can be used as a tale of morality. The histories of Helen of Troy, Cleopatra, Boudicca, Anne Boleyn, and Joan of Arc are synonymous with violence, extremism, or sex: these are the limited ways women are allowed to exist historically.[24] In that same vein, think about the impact of present-day women's movements and how some sections of society deem it an annoyance. Sister Song's "Reproductive Justice" movement, Tarana Burke's "Me Too" movement, the Women's March—we've encountered innumerable eye rolls when discussing what these movements are trying to accomplish and teach us. Society conditions women into believing they can only exist within very narrow guidelines of how to think and behave, while most men are given the full spectrum of opportunity.

It's important to note that large groups of men have also been erased from, or minimized within, the recording of our global history, mainly groups deemed to be "subordinate" like peasants or enslaved populations. Yet some of these former "subordinates" were able to rise in power, and their histories were recorded, an experience women were not afforded. As Dr. Lerner writes in *The Creation of the Patriarchy*, " ... men and women have suffered exclusion and discrimination because of their class. No man has been excluded from the historical record because of his sex, yet all women were."[25]

For some readers, it might be hard to move through this material without having a knee-jerk reaction of disbelief which can close you off to what we're discussing. The thing we need you to remember is that we've all been raised within a patriarchal construct, so those beliefs are well and truly ingrained in all of us, and just to confirm: the Patriarchy is not quiet. It will always speak up when it's threatened. Any time you have a visceral reaction or burning drive to dismiss what we're talking about, take note of where it's coming from—it's probably not your own voice that you're hearing.

How we have internalized the Patriarchy is reflective of how it has evolved within our changing societies. While most of us have been raised to believe in the neutrality of scientific research, by looking to the past we can see that many prominent scientific theories, some of which are alive and well today, reflect and promote the Patriarchy on a grand scale. Sigmund Freud, famed psychologist of the late nineteenth and early twentieth centuries, believed that when little girls discovered they had "inferior" genitals, the clitoris being an undeveloped penis (cue the world's biggest eye roll), they felt shame and "penis envy," which "turned them feminine." This meant that girls would then go on to display the "normal" feminine traits of vanity, envy, compromised intelligence, masochism, repressed libido, and stunted emotional growth. Freud also believed that femininity was both a deficient disease and a damaged form of masculinity.[26] It's also important to note that Freud believed the only "proper" form of orgasm for a woman to engage in was vaginal, and that clitoral (or any other type) of orgasm was "psychotic" or "infantile."[27]

Isn't it incredible that the proclaimed "Founder of Psychoanalysis,"[28] who has been passed down to us with so much reverence, was, in fact, a rampant misogynist who spread false and hugely damaging rhetoric disguised as scientific truth? Equally dumbfounding is how his teachings have been accepted into the modern vernacular and that they are still being taught today when he clearly harbored deeply foundational misogyny. Some might say that we shouldn't use a modern lens when looking at the past, but there were opponents of Freud's work as it was being produced.

Karen Horney, a contemporary of Freud's, loudly rejected his theories and brought forward her own, which included the claiming of the clitoris as an integral feature of a woman's sexuality. She inverted Freud's theory of penis envy into a woman's envy of men's social status, which was a recognition of the social disadvantage women experience in adulthood. Horney went on to describe a phenomenon of an intense envy that men had of pregnancy, childbirth, and lactation, which she had extensively documented and called "womb envy." Cisgender men were jealous of the incredible power of creating and sustaining new life and felt the need to overvalue their achievements and skills while debasing women in an effort to be less threatened by them. Predictably, Freud dismissed Horney's theory of womb envy as a result of Horney's own penis envy.[29]

So how does the Patriarchy influence how we live today? It's the reason why the word "man" is used to describe both a man and the human species as a whole and why, in gender-inflected languages like French, Spanish, and Italian, a group of women is feminine until you add in a single man and then the entire group becomes masculine. It's why car safety mechanisms are based on the measurements of the "average man" and result in 47 percent more women dying in car accidents than men.[30] It's why women make up only 24 percent of the people seen, heard, or read about in major media outlets, from newspapers to television.[31] It's why men are the central characters in American textbooks 57 percent of the time versus women's 31 percent, which is trounced by the UK and China's almost unbelievable rate of 87 percent male to female characters.[32] It's also why in 2018, only 18 percent of video games starred women as the central character.[33] It's why women and men are allocated equal amounts of space in public toilets despite women taking two-thirds longer than a man to use the restroom. This is in part due to the impact of menstruation that many of us deal with, the fact that women tend to be primary caregivers and may have children with them, and the fact that women make up the majority of the aged population globally and require more time.[34] Hence the ubiquitous line leading into every women's public toilet around the world. It's why women experience more pressure than men when they buy a new car, negotiate a lease, or secure a mortgage despite controlling 85 percent of all purchases made and with a massive shift of assets to women of $30 trillion expected by 2030.[35]

All of the above (and more) take place daily, nearly five millennia on from the rise of militant tribalism because our social construct was based on the patriarchal foundation that men are primary and women are secondary, that a woman's existence is a "niche" experience or perspective. Before it starts to sound like men are reaping huge rewards from the Patriarchy, it needs to be said that even though the Patriarchy is set up for men to benefit from it, it damages them as well.

"Toxic masculinity" is a term that gets bandied about in the media, but what does it really mean? In essence, it's the perception of what it is to be a man within a patriarchal society, and its stranglehold on men's emotional maturity and communication skills is a key reason why suicide is the biggest killer of men under the age of forty-five in the UK[36] and globally affects people who indentify as men twice as much as people who identify as women.[37] The poison of toxic masculinity comes from its foundation on the Patriarchy's flawed basis of gender as binary and its creation, application, and adherence to strict gender roles and stereotypes. Men are expected to stick to the "masculine" markers of being strong and unemotional, whereas a "feminine" woman must be soft and nurturing. Men are decision-makers, and women are supportive caretakers, and we see these roles assigned to children from a very young age. Girls are trained to be kind, emotive, and quiet, while boys are deterred from displaying emotions like sadness or fear and are encouraged to loudly explore their world. Boys are taught that crying is a weakness, and girls are taught that being assertive is the same as being aggressive, neither of which are good (for girls). Extra care and caution are taken over a girl's appearance and safety; her father will be warned that he'll have to "fight off the men" when she's older. Boys are wryly celebrated for being troublemakers, and men joke that daughters will have to be "locked up" for their own protection once they grow up. These identities are rigidly applied to all children, and those who can exist within these boundaries are deemed to be acceptable, while those who cannot (or will not) are punished, alienated, and pushed to the fringes.

This oppressive structure has created a society where we live our lives in line with specific gender roles: men are doctors and women are nurses; men are pilots and women are flight attendants; men are directors and women are secretaries. In predominantly male workplaces like construction, information technology, law, and medicine, there is a preponderance of men in key leadership roles while women tend to be employed in support roles like administration or human resources.[38] When women do find their way into positions that men traditionally hold, there tends to be an initial backlash typified by isolation and alienation before a hazing process is conducted where the woman is constantly tested for strength of will, skill, intelligence, and whether she can "hang with the guys." If she manages to pass the initial hazing stage, there will be more hurdles to come as each time she meets or works with a new man uninitiated to her position as a woman in a "man's world," she'll have to prove herself all over again. In fact, she'll have to demonstrate her worth, strength, and the fact that she deserves to exist in *their* environment each and every time she comes into contact with a new man, whether this man is a client or a colleague. It's easy to understand why working women are more likely to suffer burnout and burnout at a faster rate than their male counterparts.[39]

The Patriarchy also shapes our unconscious conditioning, the subconscious beliefs we acquire over a lifetime that impact our attitudes, actions, and decision-making. This conditioning is deeply impacted by existing in a social construct predominantly controlled by White, nondisabled, cisgender, heterosexual men. Our conditioning can be in direct opposition to our declared beliefs; they could potentially oppose each other as our conditioning tends to sit outside of our conscious awareness. We can, and do, hold discriminatory conditioning about other people, ranging from their race and gender to their age, sexual orientation, appearance, and body size. They come from a lifetime of exposure to both direct and indirect messages received from our families, the media, and shaped by our lived experiences. This discriminatory conditioning will generally favor the group we originate from or are "controlled by," though we can also hold conditioning against our "own group" too. The bad news is that you probably hold a lot more discriminatory conditioning than you thought you would: one way to check is to run through any of the fifteen tests run by Project Implicit, developed at Harvard University, and see what is being flagged by your reactions so that you can investigate it further.[40] The good news is that our discriminatory conditioning can be unlearned if we're willing to do the work. It's only holding you back from being the greatest possible version of yourself, so why wouldn't you want to learn how to lay it down and leave it behind? There is no better time than now.

After reading all of that, if you're anything like us, you're probably wondering why such an inequitable social construct that was created so long ago still exists. How is it still relevant in the face of our many social and technological evolutions since that time? Academic and activist Dorothy Dinnerstein says that human beings are "freaks of nature" who continually evolve in order to efficiently function within an environment that we modify with each new invention and revolution. By our very nature, we have to reinvent ourselves and our environments in order to survive, something we have historically been doing in a way that threatens our planet's survival and is poisonously oppressive, all for the sake of upholding masculine weaponry and technology.[41] So why have we not evolved past the Patriarchy?

First, because it's so omnipresent that it's essentially invisible. Most of us have to see something to know that it is there. Like systemic racism, the Patriarchy is the water that we all swim in, so we have to retrain our eyes to see that what we have been referring to as the status quo is actually the Patriarchy. You have to name the thing to know the thing.

Second, because the Patriarchy is built into the foundation of our social construct, when you speak against it, the backlash is often swift and cruel. If, for instance, you try to talk about the gender pay gap, many people will tell you that it doesn't exist and point to articles, often scholarly and intelligent, denying the experiences of the majority of women in the workplace. Perhaps you want to discuss why women have been systematically ignored for the majority of our shared social history. In that case, you'll be bombarded by ideologies dressed up as truisms claiming that a woman's biological place has always been in the home and not on the battlefield or the throne, "where history is made." If you say that you don't believe a woman should be expected to take a man's name after marriage, you'll be considered a man-hating feminazi. These kinds of discussions trigger the patriarchal conditioning of many people, whether learned or subconsciously absorbed, and the knee-jerk impulse is to regurgitate the misogyny we've all been taught by both school and society.

We can't change the world overnight, and a swift removal of the Patriarchy from our social construct would be very difficult to accomplish, not least because it would require a simultaneous global enlightenment. As that seems highly unlikely, there are a few key things that we can all do on a daily basis that will help to break its hold.

How Not to be a Tool (of the Patriarchy):

1. **Check your language.** Do you use the word "mankind," "policeman," or call your friends "gay" as a joke? This kind of language is tied to the Patriarchy. Practice using non-gender-specific descriptors like "humankind" and "police officer" and understand that queer identities as well as identities existing outside of the gender binary are both natural and ancient—we have records of them dating back millennia across most cultures; they just weren't included in Westernized "Euro-centric" school curriculums. Check out PBS's Map of Gender Diverse Cultures[42] and look at the work of Alok Vaid-Menon (@alokvmenon), author of the excellent *Beyond the Gender Binary*,[43] to start your gender diversity educational journey.

2. **Don't accept the status quo.** Just because the world works in a certain way now does not mean it's how it should be. In the past, people have been legally enslaved. It was illegal to be gay, marry someone of a different race to your own, or for anyone other than White men to own property. Speak up when someone communicates or behaves in a way that supports a patriarchal ideology—as uncomfortable as it may be, you're doing them a favor in the long run.

3. **Lose the idea of gender as binary.** Boys are not blue, and girls are not pink; boys can (and should) cry, and girls are strong; boys can be ballerinas, and girls can drive monster trucks. We like to imagine that gender is a scale of both male and female, so people can be whatever mixture of each feels right for them. Do what you have to do in order to understand that "normality" is much bigger than an exclusionary binary system: we recommend reading Cade Hildreth's illuminating breakdown of gender as bimodal instead of binary.[44]

4. **Learn.** Study the things that interest, or don't sound right, to you. Don't know anything about the different cultures of the African continent in prehistory because you weren't taught about them in school? Don't know anything about the role of women in ancient society outside of them existing in the home? Look it up, buy books, take courses, learn about all of it. There are incredible resources available on just about any subject your mind can conjure up; you just have to be willing to put the time in to do the research and expand your knowledge. Kofi Annan said, "Knowledge is power. Information is liberating. Education is the premise of progress, in every society, in every family."[45] Nothing could be more accurate, and with knowledge comes change.

To learn more, please check out these additional resources:

Books

- Bates, Laura. *Everyday Sexism*. New York: Thomas Dunne Books, 2016.
- Frances-White, Deborah. *The Guilty Feminist*. London: Virago Press, 2018.
- Gay, Roxane. *Bad Feminist*. London: Corsair, 2014.
- Given, Florence. *Women Don't Owe You Pretty*. Kansas City, Missouri: Andrews McMeel Publishing, 2021.
- Lerner, Gerda. *The Creation of Patriarchy*. Oxford: Oxford University Press, 1986.

Activists/ Influencers

- Claire_Training *she/her*
  - Instagram @claire_training @ScienceWithClaire
  - TikTok @claire_training @ScienceWithClaire
- Farida D.
  - Instagram @farida.d.author
  - www.faridad.com
- Feminist
  - Instagram @feminist
  - www.feministforall.carrd.co
- Fuck Patriarchy
  - Instagram @fuck_patriarchy
- Heb *she/her*
  - Instagram @HebOntheWeb
  - TikTok @HebOntheWeb
- SisterSong
  - Instagram @sistersong_woc
- The Solidarity Sisters *she/her/hers*
  - Instagram @thesolidaritysisters
- Yeet the Patriarchy *she/her*
  - Instagram @a_tired_feminist

CHAPTER 4
LOOKING THROUGH CONCRETE WALLS

You may encounter many defeats, but you must not
be defeated. It may be necessary to encounter the defeats,
so you can know who you are, what you can rise from,
how you can still come out of it.

–MAYA ANGELOU

N o matter where in the world you live, you're constantly surrounded by stereotypes. They change depending on where you live and the environment you're raised in, including the influence of family, society, and media. In principle, stereotypes are meant to be an objective mental index of what you will encounter in your daily life in order to ensure your survival: babies cry, dogs bark, and birds fly. Unfortunately, the most powerful and pervasive stereotypes are drawn from derogatory social narratives, and they perpetuate the belief that certain people are "favored" and others are "unfavored." These stereotypes taint our perception of people who look and act differently from us. Many stereotypes were intentionally created to make people "fit the narrative" that our social construct is built upon, one that is both divisive and oppressive in nature. In the corporate world, where systemic racism and our patriarchal social construct intersect, the results are, unsurprisingly, that Black people and people of Color are overwhelmingly penalized just for walking through the door and looking "different."

The corporate world rejects Black women and women of Color for both their gender *and* their race, so they suffer doubly, and the stereotypes about them are as deeply entrenched in the workplace as they are in society: the angry Black woman; the docile, obedient Asian woman; the feisty, loud Latina. Sound familiar? In a job interview, women from these communities are judged in ways that most White women would not think twice about, like how their attire or hairstyle plays a serious factor in whether they are deemed to be "employable." If your hair is in an afro or you're wearing a hijab, then chances are you could be passed over for a job because of the way you look, not your ability to do the job. Just securing the interview will be more difficult if the name on your resume is not White-sounding.

These markers are part of a discriminatory phenomenon defined by Evelyn Brooks Higginbotham, author and Harvard professor of African American Studies, as "respectability politics": the policing of Black people and people of Color into presenting themselves as more "White."[46] It's one of the reasons why natural hairstyles like afros, locs, or dreads have historically been considered inappropriate for a corporate setting and why, since the Court of Justice of the European Union (CJEU) decision of 2017, a woman working in Europe can legally be fired for wearing a head covering at work. It's why some Black women and women of Color feel pressured to shorten their names or have a work nickname, including Minda Harts, author of *The Memo: What Women of Color Need to Know to Secure a Seat at the Table.*[47] Born Yassminda, Harts felt that putting her full name on her resume would hurt her chances of being brought in for an interview and decided to shorten it to Minda. She speaks in *The Memo* about this decision being part of "a vicious cycle of making [W]hite people feel comfortable with me being Black at work."[48]

Harts had every reason to fear that her full, "ethnic" sounding name might impact her ability to secure an interview. A study done by the Centre for Social Investigation in the UK showed that applicants with names that sounded like they were from a "minority ethnic" background but with the same qualifications and experience as applicants with "White-sounding" names had to send 60 percent more applications before receiving a similar response.[49] A two-year study conducted in the United States by Katherine Decelles and Sonia K. Kang showed that companies were twice as likely to call applicants from Black and Brown communities if they "Whitened" their resumes.[50] Unfortunately, once a Black woman or woman of Color gets the job, their on-the-job experience doesn't necessarily improve.

There was a ground-breaking intersectional study carried out in the 1990s by Ella L.J.E. Bell Smith, professor at Dartmouth's Tuck School of Business, and Stella Nkomo, professor at the University of Pretoria, on women and intersectionality in the corporate world, which researched the lives and career struggles of White and Black women.[51] The women included in the study were part of the first wave of female managers of the 1970s and 1980s and were given, mainly due to the gains made by the civil rights movement, access to new educational opportunities and were able to enter careers that were not traditionally accepting of women, Black people, and people of Color. Surveying more than 800 women over eight years, Smith and Nkomo asked about their specific childhood supports and obstacles, as well as what sacrifices they had had to make in early adulthood to achieve their career standings. These lines of inquiry were used to gain an understanding of the real issues separating the experiences of women who came from different racial backgrounds. Their findings were manifold, but there was a key starting point: White women were not told as children that there would be a difference in their achievements compared to men's when they reached the corporate world. They mistook the gender discrimination they encountered as a corporate issue or assumed it was just how the business world worked. The majority of Black women were told as children to expect racism and discriminatory behavior, so they were prepared for the obstacles that a workplace constructed for, and dominated by, White men would raise against them.

Through their research, Smith and Nkomo found that White men were more willing to share strategic company information, including insights on internal politics and culture, with White women which enabled them to gain a strategic foothold within the corporate structure. The research went on to find that White women tended to only share this information with their White colleagues, which was a huge inhibitor of the career progression of Black women. Smith and Nkomo's research indicated that instead of there being a "glass ceiling," a phrase used in reference to the invisible barrier that often keeps White women from advancing in the corporate world, Black women were facing a "concrete wall." The advantage of the glass ceiling was that while a White woman was obstructed from upward movement, they were still able to be seen within the company's context, and that ceiling could potentially be shattered. Black women were kept in the background, behind a wall that they could not see through, nor could their skillsets and abilities be distinguished as long as they were kept behind it. Additionally, the women kept behind this concrete wall had no idea what they could expect to find on the other side, so they were unprepared for further success if they did manage to make their way over it. Smith and Nkomo shared an excellent description of this experience from one of the women they interviewed, who explained it as feeling like a guest in someone else's house despite being there for years. These feelings of exclusion were ubiquitous throughout her working career, and ultimately, were never resolved.[52]

This holds true today with Black women and women of Color still working behind a concrete wall and, in general, receiving less support from their managers than their White colleagues. This lack of support manifests as work contributions not being shared with key management or directors, little or no assistance in navigating organizational politics, and managers or directors tending not to socialize with Black women and women of Color outside the work environment. All this despite 83 percent of Asian women, 80 percent of Black women, and 76 percent of Latina women saying they want to be promoted, compared to 68 percent of White women.[53] Because so many Black women and women of Color feel their skills are not celebrated or even understood, they struggle to build key relationships within their companies. The findings of Smith and Nkomo's study suggested that Black women found it more advantageous to leave a company for another in order to gain the visibility they so desperately needed in order to progress their careers.[54]

These facts have a deep impact on both the professional and personal lives of women of Color, particularly Black women, as they tend to be the main breadwinners for their families when compared to their White female colleagues. A 2020 report by the Institute for Women's Policy Research confirmed that 74 percent of Black mothers in the US are their household's main earner compared to 41 percent of Asian women, 45 percent of White women, 47 percent of Latina women, and 58 percent of Indigenous women, most of whom were employed in nursing, care work, and teaching professions.[55] This kind of data, separated by both gender and race, is harder to pin down for the UK and Europe, but what we do know is that in the UK, 28 percent of women are the main breadwinners for their families,[56] while in Europe it is 31.4 percent.[57] Maternal breadwinners tend to be from low and middle-income households and are overwhelmingly employed in health, education, and social work. Statistics from the Equality and Human Rights Commission (EHRC's) Race Report show that Pakistani, Bangladeshi, and Black adults are more likely to live in "substandard accommodation" than White people[58] and and that 46 percent of Black, Asian, and "ethnic minority" children currently live in poverty compared to 26 percent of White children.[59] The UK government's white paper *Ethnicity, Gender, and Social Mobility* reported that Black women and women of Color are concentrated in the teaching, childcare, nursing, and care sectors, with Black Caribbean women typically working in the health and social care sectors.[60] By extrapolating the available data, we can see that the situation in Europe, and more specifically the UK, is comparable to what's happening in the US.

There is a well-known statistic that women earn 82 cents for every dollar that a man earns for the same work, but this statistic is an average of all reported earnings for American women against all reported earnings for American men. White women in the US earn 79 cents on average to every dollar earned by a White man while Black women earn 63 cents, Indigenous women earn 60 cents, and Latina women earn 55 cents. Asian American and Pacific Islander women (AAPI) tend to suffer the least pay disparity at 85 cents on average to a White man's dollar, though there is a wide variance of earnings from the manifold ethnicities included within the AAPI community so this average earning statistic can be misleading.[61]

In the UK, White men are typically out-earned by both Chinese and Indian men, but if we use the average hourly earnings of a White man, £13.37, as our measuring stick to maintain parity with the US statistics, women from all backgrounds earn at least £1.34 less than they do per hour, with the single exception of Chinese women who earn £1.36 more per hour. The women who earn the least are Pakistani women at £3.76 less per hour, Bangladeshi women (who out-earn Bangladeshi men by 95 pence) at £3.37 less, and Black British, Black African, and Black Caribbean women at £2.74 less.[62] The extremity of this disparity is particularly disturbing when you also know that at least a third of these women are supporting entire households on their income. In the US, the majority of Black women are the main financial support of their families, earning 39 percent on average less than a White man does, with their Latina and Indigenous female colleagues suffering even greater disparity.[63] This makes the tendency of their White female colleagues not to actively support the progression of Black women and women of Color in the workplace even more damning.

Why would White women do so little to assist Black women and women of Color when we are all ostensibly "fighting the same fight" against gender inequality? In her influential essay, "White Privilege and Male Privilege," Peggy McIntosh, author and senior research scientist of the Wellesley Centers for Women, broke down many of the damaging tropes that allowed White people to perpetuate racism in the workplace, and the wider world. She discussed how lightly the enslavement of African people is taught in schools, that only those who were enslaved were seen as dehumanized or at risk of dehumanization, and that there was no focus on the damaged mentality of the enslavers. She discussed how racism wasn't actively "unlearned" by White enslavers when the American civil war ended; there was no "deep dive" into what it did to a person's moral code when they had been allowed to "own" another person or how damaging a belief White supremacy is and how hard it is to uproot and destroy. White children were not—and still aren't—taught that White people have historically been the oppressor and given unfair advantages within the construct of a society whose foundation is based on racism and, therefore, deeply flawed. White children were and—again, still are—taught to believe that their lives are morally neutral and their experiences are the "norm." It allows the perpetuation of the idea that all those who work hard should be able to attain a "White" lifestyle. McIntosh believes that if White children were taught the truth about their cultural history, they would realize these deep-seated ideas are enormously flawed and the ideas that Western countries are "free countries" and that success based on hard work alone is possible (i.e., meritocracy) are myths.[64]

While it is important to note that many of these beliefs are achieved through ignorance, McIntosh rightly says that to be oblivious to one's privilege is an incrimination itself. White, or light, skin gives an unearned societal privilege that White people are conditioned to believe is normal, and McIntosh's White privilege checklist, paraphrased below, counts the ways in which white skin confers benefits to its owner.[65]

Hidden in Plain Sight—Recognizing White Privilege:

1. White people can, if they want to, be in the company of other White people most of the time.
2. White people can choose to avoid spending time with people of other races, whom they have been conditioned to mistrust and who, in response, have probably learned to mistrust White people.
3. White people have little trouble renting or purchasing housing in an area they can afford and want to live in.
4. White people can be fairly confident that when they move, their new neighbors will be nice or, at the very least, neutral to them.
5. White people can shop on their own and not be followed or harassed by store security.
6. White people consistently see other White people widely and positively represented on TV, in magazines or newspapers, and on social media.
7. When White people are taught about their cultural heritage or "civilization," they are shown that White people made it what it is.
8. White children will be taught a school curriculum that predominantly focuses on the existence and experiences of their race.
9. White writers can be pretty sure of finding a publisher for their work.

10. White people in a mixed group are typically listened to, even if there is only one White person present.
11. White people in a mixed group can choose whether or not to listen to another woman's voice if she is the only member of her race.
12. White people can consistently find the writing of their race represented in book shops, find their staple foods in a grocery store, and find someone who can competently take care of their hair in a salon.
13. When White people use checks, credit cards, or cash, their skin color is not a marker of whether or not they're financially reliable.
14. White people can consistently protect their children from people who might not like them.
15. White people don't have to educate their children to be aware of systemic racism for their own daily physical protection.
16. White people can be confident that their children's teachers and employers will tolerate them if they fit school and workplace norms; their main concern isn't other people's attitudes toward their race.
17. White people can behave "impolitely" (i.e., talk with their mouths full of food, interrupt others, shout in public) and not have people associate this with their skin color.
18. White people can swear, wear second-hand clothes, and not answer letters/emails, without having these choices attributed to the bad morals, the poverty, or the illiteracy of their race.
19. White people can speak in public to a powerful male group without having their race put on trial.
20. White people can do well in a challenging situation without being called a credit to their race.

21. White people are never asked to speak for the actions of their racial group.
22. White people can be oblivious to the languages and customs of the world's majority without experiencing a penalty.
23. White people can criticize their government and talk about their fear of its policies without being seen as a cultural outsider.
24. White people who ask to speak to "the person in charge," will probably face another White person.
25. White people can be sure that if they've been pulled over by the police or chosen for a tax audit, it's not because of their race.
26. White people can easily find and buy books, greeting cards, toys, and magazines featuring other White people.
27. White people tend to feel tied in, rather than isolated or feared in most meetings at the companies they work for.
28. White people who argue with a colleague of another race are less likely to experience a career penalty for it than their colleague will.
29. White people can argue for the promotion of a person of another race, or a program centering on race, without experiencing a career penalty, even if their colleagues disagree with them.
30. White people who express that there is, or isn't, a racial issue going on, will be deemed more credible for either position than a Black person or person of Color.
31. White people can choose to ignore or engage with developments in the activism of Black communities and communities of Color, without experiencing negative consequences of either choice.
32. White people are not taught to fear what ignoring the perspectives and lived experiences of people of other races says about them.

33. White people's body shape, bearing, or body odor will not be taken as a reflection on their race.
34. White people can worry about racism without being seen as self-interested or self-seeking.
35. White people can take a job with an affirmative action employer without their coworkers suspecting that they got it because of their race.
36. White people do not need to examine every negative episode or situation of a bad day, week, or year and decide whether it has racial overtones.
37. White people can be sure of finding people willing to advise them on their career path.
38. White people can consider personal or professional options without asking whether a person of their race would be accepted or allowed to do what they want to do.
39. White people can be late to a meeting without having their lateness reflect on their race.
40. White people can book a hotel or other public accommodation without fearing that people of their race can't get in or will be mistreated because of their race.
41. White people can be sure that if they need legal or medical help, their race won't work against them.
42. White people can arrange their lives so that they never have to experience feelings of rejection due to their race.
43. White people who are rated poorly as a leader can be sure that their race is not the problem.
44. White people can easily find academic courses and institutions that give attention only to people of their race.
45. White people can expect the language and imagery in all of the arts to speak to the experiences of their race.
46. White people can choose medical bandages, makeup, hosiery, shoes, and clothes in "flesh color" or "nude" and have them more or less match their skin.[66]

There are very few items, if any, on this list that capture actions or attitudes that are outside of our everyday existence. They relate to what we buy, how we eat, how we talk, how we dress, the minutiae that make up our daily lives. Many White women are unaware that their assumption that a store will carry foundation, bandages, or hosiery matching their skin color and hair care products suitable for use on their hair is a privilege. As White women, we know that by ignoring this privilege, we are expressing our own our own racist conditioning, covert as it may feel. Acknowledging our inherent, learned racism is not only necessary; it's natural. We have all been raised in a systemically discriminatory society, which means we have all absorbed an inordinate amount of negative conditioning. Unfortunately, admitting this truth has been held up as a shameful thing to many of us. Saying you're not racist is popular among White people, something to loudly exclaim whenever we feel like our moral code is being called into question.

The common misconception about racism is that because most White people don't outwardly express explicitly racist sentiment, we're not racist—but the fact is that all White people benefit from racism and have done so for centuries. While we didn't directly participate in the enslavement of others and we don't publicly espouse racist ideology, we are all accomplices. We may not pull a "Becky" or a "Karen" and weaponize our White skin by calling the police on a Black person or person of Color, but when we stay silent in the face of racist speech or actions, we are accomplices. When a White person says that they don't see color, that too is a negation of the experiences of Black people and people of Color in a systemically racist society, and that, too, makes us accomplices.

The lasting problem of racism is that because White people are so bad at talking about it and owning their roles in its perpetuation, we can't find ways for all of us, oppressors and those being oppressed, to move past it. When White people do talk about race and feel discomfort (like when they're called out for perpetuating racism), many are unable to handle feeling uncomfortable. They react emotionally with tears, anger, or guilt. This is also why many White people won't correct other White people on covert racism; we're always trying to keep the peace and not rock the boat. One of the best pieces of camouflage that racism has developed is that it's binary: you're either a confederate-flag toting Nazi sympathizer, or a good person who believes in equity. So when you, a kind, compassionate person, are presented with the evidence that you are complicit in systemic racial discrimination, the disbelief and extreme defensiveness (along with the tears, anger, or guilt) are all part of the systems and structures that allow racism to retain its foothold in society unchecked. We include ourselves in this; White people need to recognize their internalized racism, do the work to unlearn what we have *all* been taught, and work hard to support Black people and people of Color every day, in both the wider world as well as in the workplace. In the words of the educator Jane Elliott, "You are not born racist. You are born into a racist society. And like anything else, if you can learn it, you can unlearn it."[67]

In *The Memo*, Minda Harts speaks about there being a limited number of seats in the boardroom for women, and even fewer for Black women and women of Color.[68] Did you know that before 2021, there was only one Black woman CEO of a Fortune 500 company? Ursula Burns, CEO of Xerox, has been on Forbes's 100 Most Powerful Women in the World list several times; she was one of Hilary Clinton's potential candidates for vice president. She should, at the very least, be internationally lauded, but have you ever heard her name before? How about Rosalind "Roz" Brewer, CEO of Walgreens Boots, or Thasunda Brown Duckett, CEO of the Teachers Insurance and Annuity Association of America (TIAA), formerly a CEO of Chase Consumer Banking? These women are the only Black female CEOs of Fortune 500 companies in the history of the list, and while most readers won't know their names, pretty much everyone knows who Sheryl Sandberg is. Do you think that's because Sheryl Sandberg has achieved more than Ursula Burns, Roz Brewer, or Thasunda Brown Duckett in the corporate environment? Or is it because the media tends to focus on and make a bigger deal out of White women's success? Is it any surprise when we see how the odds are stacked against success for Black women and women of Color in the corporate workplace? Fixing this disparity will require systemic change and concerted effort on the part of everyone, but it cannot in any way be shifted onto the shoulders of the women affected by this. Black women and women of Color should not be given any more work to do—White people, White *women* specifically, need to become better partners in the workplace, and it needs to start *today*.

To Minda Harts, this means people with authority doing more to partner with people who do not look like or identify the same way as they do and helping them find and secure an accelerated career track. Harts tells the story of when she asked a White female executive whether she would prefer to hire a woman with a natural hairstyle, like an afro, or a ponytail. The woman replied that she and most board members would always hire the woman with the ponytail. She went on to tell Harts that though she knew it wasn't fair, companies only wanted "clean-cut women of Color." This woman had the influence and clout to change this racist corporate culture, but she wouldn't risk stepping out of line or rocking the boat and demanding equity. Unfortunately, this falls in line with the research Harts has done among the women who attend her workshops, over 90 percent of whom say that their biggest champions and supporters in the workplace are White men while White women have done little to support them.[69]

White women: we can see that the corporate world is neither diverse nor equitable, and we need to be actively supporting Black women and women of Color in the workplace. If you're placed to do so (i.e., a director, executive, etc.), you need to be looking out for Black women and women of Color who want mentorship and/or sponsorship in your workplace. Sponsorship requires you to learn about someone's career goals, help them formulate a plan to achieve those goals, and then support them in that process. This can be done by assisting them in building a stronger work network and putting them forward within the company for promotion or new opportunities. Mentors act as a professional support system, offering mentees career advice, amplifying their skill set if it's being overlooked, or just holding a safe, supportive space for them on hard days. Both of these sets of actions will create strong working bonds and increase the diversity of every team (which is statistically supported as directly relating to a company's ability to create) they are applied to as well as genuinely supporting the hard-working women who much of the time are being ignored within the status quo of the corporate world.[70] To be clear, this should not come from a place of "White saviorship." White women do not need to "save" Black women and women of Color; they just need to show up for them in the same way that they would for a White colleague. That's it.

If, like us, you're a White woman, then we cannot say that we believe in racial equity and then restrict it to just nodding and smiling when we pass a Black woman or woman of Color in the office hallway. Making the minimum effort while toeing the corporate company line, which is based on both a racist and patriarchal system of control and oppression, has been done for too long and is only making a bad situation worse. The writer James Baldwin said, "I can't believe what you say because I see what you do,"[71] and we as women, who already experience oppression, cannot be complicit in, or contribute to, the continued oppression of Black women and women of Color simply because it makes us uncomfortable to engage in conflict. Reach out, use your voice, do your part to help demolish that concrete wall.

The White Woman's Starter Kit for Being a Better Success Partner in the Workplace:

1. **Educate yourself about racism.** This is not a one-time thing; it's not "one and done." This is a continual, evolving process that you will need to engage in for the rest of your life. And yes, it's exhausting, emotional work to do. If you're only just starting, consider yourself lucky that you've been able to live as long as you have without doing the work because you could look away and experience no penalty for doing so. Black women and women of Color have been exhausted by the realities of racism for their entire lives. For them, it's inescapable; for you, it's a choice to engage with it. So please make that choice every day.

2. **Listen.** When a Black woman or woman of Color corrects you or tells you that you've been offensive, LISTEN. Don't impatiently wait for your turn to talk. Don't cry or use emotional weaponry to shift power back to yourself. You made a mistake, and they are doing you a favor by educating you. You are not owed that education. Thank them for it, apologize, and learn from the moment.

3. **Do not centralize yourself.** This is not about you. This is about racism. Misogyny and sexism are debilitating to experience in the workplace and the wider world, but they do not compare to the experiences of racial discrimination. You do not need to be the winner of the Most Oppressed Person Award, nor should you even want to earn that title.

4. **Reject the pull of White saviorship.** White saviorship is the belief that because you're White, you know what's best for everyone. A White savior assumes that anyone who isn't White is somehow lacking, and that White people are best placed to advocate for them. This happens by speaking over or "for" someone else, by attempting to control the career

path or advocate for someone without their expressed permission, or by infantilizing someone because you believe you're more competent to make decisions on their behalf. As we said above, all that is needed from you in the workplace is to propagate the same advocacy for Black women and women of Color that you do for White women.

5. **Don't leave your activism on the internet.** Use your voice in the workplace, on the streets, and at home. Do not let uncomfortable or inappropriate comments slide. It will be uncomfortable in the moment to let someone know they've upset you, but it needs to be done. That includes when you see or hear discriminatory language or microaggressions toward others; the people affected by these behaviors need to see and hear your support to feel safe around you. And that is the most important part of all of this work: letting Black women and women of Color know, with actions not just words, that you are doing your utmost to create a safe space for them in the workplace.

If you want to learn more about divesting yourself (and your company) from White-centricity, here are educators who are helping us to unlearn racism and evolve into something greater:

- Layla Saad, *Me and White Supremacy*
- Ijeoma Oluo, *So You Want to Talk about Race*
- Ruby Hamad, *White Tears/ Brown Scars*
- Reni Eddo-Lodge, *Why I'm No Longer Talking to White People about Race*
- Michelle Alexander, *The New Jim Crow*
- Isabel Wilkerson, *Caste*
- Ibram X. Kendi, *How to be Antiracist* and *Stamped*
- Alicia Garza, *The Purpose of Power*
- Rachel Cargle, *The Great Unlearn*
- Mikki Kendall, *Hood Feminism*

- Afua Hirsch, *Brit(ish)*
- Koa Beck, *White Feminism*

To learn more, please check out these additional resources:

Books

- Dabiri, Emma. *What White People Can Do Next: From Allyship to Coalition.* New York: Harper Perennial, 2021. (Dabiri 2021)
- Hannah-Jones, Nikole, and Renée Watson. *The 1619 Project.* New York: Random House Publishing Group, 2021.
- Hawthorne, Britt. Raising Anti-Racist Children: A Practical Parenting Guide. (Hawthorne 2022)
- Jackson, Regina and Rao, Saira. White Women: Everything You Already Know About Your Own Racism and How to Do Better. (Penguin, 2022)
- Reid, Nova. *The Good Ally: A Guided Anti-Racism Journey from Bystander to Changemaker.* London: HQ, 2021.

Activists/ Influencers

- Ally Henny
  - Instagram @allyhenny
  - www.thearmchaircommentary.com
- Angel Jones, PhD *she/her*
  - Instagram @angeljonesphd
  - www.angeljonesphd.com
- Check Your Privilege
  - Instagram @ckyourprivilege
  - www.checkyourprivilege.co/ig

- Conscious Lee *he/him/they*
  - Instagram @theconsciouslee
  - www.GeorgeLeeSpeaks.com
- Dr. Jaiya John
  - Instagram @jaiyajohn
  - www.jaiyajohn.com
- Dr. Shola Mos-Shogbamimu
  - Instagram @sholamos1
  - Twitter @Sholamos1
- Luvvie Ajayi Jones
  - Instagram @luvvie
  - Instagram @LuvvNation
  - www.luvvnation.com
- Lynae Vanee
  - Instagram @_lyneezy
  - TikTok @_lyneezy
- Privilegetoprogress
  - Instagram @privtoprog
- Race 2 Dinner
  - Instagram @race2dinner
  - www.race2dinner.com
- Sue Yun *she/her/hers*
  - Instagram @hisueyun

CHAPTER 5
YOU CAN'T HAVE IT ALL

Because I am a woman, I must make unusual efforts to succeed. If I fail, no one will say, "She doesn't have what it takes." They will say, "Women don't have what it takes."
–Clare Boothe Luce

Lisa's Story:

For as long as I've been in the construction industry, there has been one company that I always wanted to work for. To me, they were the gold standard for main contractors working not just in the UK, but globally as well. The projects they complete are renowned throughout the world for their uniqueness and the build skill required to complete them.

After I had my son and came back to work when he was eleven months old, I found myself wanting more. If I was going to be away from him for ten hours a day, then I needed my working life to be in pursuit of the highest possible ambitions that I had for myself. So, four months into my return to work, I applied for a position at the interiors division of this company that I so respected. After several interviews, to my amazement, I ended up getting the job.

In each of my interviews, I had been explicit about needing flexible working hours as I had a young son at home and wasn't *able to commit to any job that would adversely affect a healthy work-life balance. I was repeatedly promised that there would be no demands on my time that would require me to change my expectations of how my personal and my work life would intersect. My partner, who also works in construction, had reservations about the job and was worried that I wasn't being given the real story about the deeply corporate, process-driven nature that thrived in multinational companies and the strain that it could potentially put on me. I remember being frustrated with him at the time: how could he think that I'd be so naïve as to not have already completely laid out my needs with the company before accepting the position? I did my best to pacify his concerns, promising that this would be the best possible thing not just for me, but for us, and I accepted the position. I could hardly believe it: I was still relatively young and I had a great partner, a beautiful son, and an incredible job at a company I had always wanted to work for. I was finally going to "have it all."*

Within a week of starting, my life began to fall apart. I realized that my expectation of what it would feel like to have it all was very different than how it actually feels to live it. Although I had been promised that a flexible working day was acceptable, the unspoken corporate expectation of our working hours was extreme. Rather than the "do your work for the day and go home" environment that I had been led to expect, my colleagues showed up to work exceedingly early and stayed long past five-thirty to demonstrate their commitment to the company, working protracted twelve- to fourteen-hour shifts every day. This could not have been more different than what was described to me during the interview process, and I felt huge pressure to come in earlier and stay far later than I had originally agreed. My first mistake was not speaking up about this as soon as I felt the pressure and expectation start to build. My second mistake was succumbing to it.

I spent the next nine weeks catching the early train out and the late train back, seeing my son for an hour each day during the work week. I took no breaks, ate at my desk, sat through back-to-back meetings that seemed to have no purpose other than to allow the meeting holder to tick a box. My previous job roles had not prepared me for the level of bureaucracy and interoffice politics that a company of this size seemed to need in order to function. I realized that the person I was—a direct result of my past work experience and having just become a mother—made my values diametrically opposed to what this company valued.

I had never believed it when I heard other women speak about the struggle to balance their work and personal lives in the pursuit of having it all. I would brush it off, knowing that when it was my turn, I could and would achieve all of my goals no matter what. Now that I "had it all," I was starting to realize that the reason I wouldn't be able to maintain it wasn't because I wasn't strong enough or smart enough. It was because many of the boxes I needed to tick to have it all were incompatible. I couldn't be both fully present as a mother and as a project manager, not just because my son's childcare setting gave me nine hours maximum a day, and my work hours were well in excess of that on a daily basis. In my eagerness to excel, I allowed the boundaries between my professional life and personal life to slip to such a point that my time at home was never free of work stress. At work, I was overwhelmed by the feeling that my career was damaging my relationship with my son.

I could have kept the job and worked those hard, long hours in order to rise in the company. My colleagues respected my skill set, and my boss told me several times that he believed I would be able to achieve whatever I wanted to in the company. But if I chose to do that, I wouldn't have been present for my son. I wouldn't have been able to drop him off at school or pick him up. I wouldn't have put him to sleep at night or woken up with him in the morning.

I would have missed so many of the infinitesimal moments of his childhood, the tiny nuances that would form him into the adult he will eventually become. Deep down, I felt that if I continued to miss all of these little moments, I wouldn't really know him as a person, and that wasn't the kind of mother I wanted to be.

I could have gone back to my old job where the expectations were much less intense, and I could be home in time to pick my son up from school and put him to bed every night. I could easily take time off to attend school plays and book extended holidays to enjoy more time with my family. The trade-off was that I wouldn't be the lead on a landmark build, I wouldn't run a large team of managers, I wouldn't help to create something new on the London skyline, which part of me still wanted. But I knew that I needed to be a visible, constant, loving presence in my son's life. I couldn't, and still can't, seem to get those two desires to balance.

I don't pretend to know what the future holds or where I'll be in five or ten years. What I do know is that I chose my son over the advancement of my career because he was, and always will be, the right choice for me. Whether I can find a way to do work that is as fulfilling as working for a top-tier company would be, I don't know. I am still pursuing something better, but I know that the choice I made was right.

Here is what breaks my heart—not the choice I made, but that I would never have had to make that choice if I was a man because a man could have had both. He would not have had to choose between taking on his dream role and having his family.

What is the biggest difference between a man and a woman when they work in the corporate world? Most women cannot make and maintain a clear separation between the responsibilities of their work life and their home life for the entirety of their careers, but men can. Why? Because they have wives, and having a wife is what ultimately sets women apart from their male colleagues.

To be clear, a wife does not have to be a cisgender woman in a heterosexual partnership. The wife we're referring to is a partner who bears a disproportionate load of the unpaid care and domestic tasks of a relationship and household, so we'll use the term "wife" for brevity's sake because that is the societal expectation of wives. In a partnership with children, a wife gets the children ready for school each morning and drops them off so that her partner can catch the early train; a wife picks the kids up from school so her partner can stay at work past 3 p.m.; a wife keeps the fridge and cupboards stocked with food and cooks dinner before putting the kids to bed so that when her partner works late, the inner workings of the house don't come to a grinding halt. As committed a partner as men can be, they are typically not the ones who pick children up from nursery or school when they get sick or hurt, nor are they the ones who stay home with kids when it's needed. Typically, men aren't the ones who book doctor and dentist appointments or remember to buy more multivitamins or toothpaste unless they are reminded (a.k.a. nagged). They may empty the trash cans, do laundry and fold clothes, maybe even load or unload the dishwasher without being reminded to do so, but everything else rests squarely on the shoulders of the wife, including the reminding. A friend of ours told us that she plans to make a book for her husband that contains all of the details that keep their home and lives running if she dies. This book, affectionately titled *If I Die*, would include monthly bill details, the children's current clothing sizes, the regularity in which household necessities should be purchased, all of the myriad minutiae that her husband blissfully ignores. Yet she is expected to be in charge of these things because she is the wife. Her idea is both funny and deeply disturbing, like most of the inequitable "facts of life" that women are expected to put up with.

For many (i.e., wives and mothers), it will come as no surprise that women do 75 percent of all unpaid care work around the world.[72] Unpaid care work can be loosely defined as everything that has to be done to keep our homes and societies running but rarely gets recognized as having merit: caring for an elderly relative, cooking and cleaning, going grocery shopping, dropping off or picking up kids from school, and looking after children. These are not optional tasks that we can choose not to do; they need to be done, and it's disproportionately women who are doing them, much of the time, in addition to paid employment. Looking at it globally, women do three times the amount of unpaid work than men, irrespective of the proportion of income they bring in.[73] As you'd expect, these tasks affect how women get through their day; women in dual-income families are twice as likely as men to include dropping off and picking up children as part of their commute. While men typically have a straightforward twice-daily commute into and out of the office, women tend to "trip-chain," which means their commute is a series of interconnected trips to schools, stores, and other places while on their way to or from work. A typical working woman with a child under five was found to have a 54 percent increase in her trip-chaining while a man's trip-chain increased by only 19 percent.[74] Even before a woman walks through the door of the office, they are bearing a heavier workload, both emotionally and physically, than their male counterparts.

How much more effective would you be at your job if you didn't have to think about whether you've run out of laundry detergent, what to make for dinner tonight, whether you have all the groceries you need, or if a housebound relative is lonely or needs to go shopping? If you have kids, are yours having too much screen time, eating a balanced diet, and getting their emotional needs met? It's considered to be the woman's role to worry about these things because men typically don't—like when a school project needs to be organized, when you buy presents for birthdays, or decide what food you'll be serving to family and friends on upcoming festive days, then buy that food, prepare it, and serve it. (And probably do the majority of the cleaning afterward.) Again, no matter how committed a partner a man may be, in the majority of cisgender heterosexual relationships, the woman is still managing the process of, and bearing the emotional load for, domestic tasks.

Mental or emotional load is the remembering, organizing, and planning that goes into making a household and a family run. It's very similar to working as a project manager; however, in the real world, a project manager is not expected to plan the work and oversee the project while simultaneously doing all of the work themselves. And therein lies the problem: women are expected to be in charge of the planning, organizing, and execution of the million-and-one domestic tasks that make up our daily lives. Unfortunately, when you balance this responsibility with paid employment outside the home, the effects on a woman's mental and physical health are disastrous.

A 2020 study by the Health and Safety Executive (HSE) found that women in the UK, at every age range, had higher rates of work-related stress, anxiety, and depression than men and were, in some age groups, experiencing twice the rate of stress as their male counterparts.[75] A woman working in paid employment between forty-one and fifty hours a week has a higher risk for developing heart disease and cancer than her male counterparts who show *less* risk of contracting heart disease or depression when working these same hours. Why? Because, typically, a man's emotional load decreases with increased working hours as he becomes less visible at home, while a women's mental load typically remains the same or expands with increased working hours.[76] She cannot become less visible; she's the one getting everything done! And yet, companies still routinely award and promote employees who can work longer hours, which does not always equate to greater dedication. This is particularly true in Japan, where promotion is based on hours worked and the length of time an employee has stayed at a company, neither of which working mothers can commit to, and leads, unsurprisingly, to 44 percent of employed

Japanese women working part-time or as temporary workers.[77] "Long hours culture" is not healthy or equitable, but data also indicates that often very little extra work is accomplished when longer hours are worked. A study by Erin Reid, professor at Boston University's Questrom School of Business, found that employers couldn't tell the difference between employees who worked eighty hours a week and those who just pretended to. Reid could also not find evidence that the employees who worked fewer hours accomplished less than their "long hours" colleagues. However, employees who made it clear that they were working fewer hours (mothers who also work outside the home, for example, and need flexibility in order to meet the demands of their unpaid care work) were penalized by their employers for doing so.[78]

Feeling tired yet? No wonder: a woman, on average, works a sixteen-hour day, and she needs a break, but even her share of leisure and relaxation time is unequal. American men have an hour more to rest each day than their female counterparts, while in the UK, men have five hours more downtime per week than women.[79] In fact, UK women aged twenty-five to thirty-four years spent 91 percent longer than men of a similar age performing unpaid work but took 10 percent less leisure time.[80] The specific memory we both share of taking a bath to de-stress and ending up with every child in the house clamoring for our attention while our partners sat downstairs watching TV uninterrupted comes to mind. Even when a woman needs to rest for medical reasons, she still has to care for others. A Finnish study found that single women recovered more quickly from heart attacks than married women because married women had to step right back into their caregiver roles—unlike single women and men, who typically had someone to look after them during their recovery, which allowed them to convalesce.[81]

Anyone who has given birth can tell you about postpartum shock: your internal organs dropping back into place, your uterus painfully shrinking after expanding to five times its original size, your breasts potentially charging themselves with milk (again, painfully), all while your hormones crash. If it was a natural birth, then chances are there's some physical trauma to heal from, especially if there have been any cuts, rips, or tears of the vagina, labia, or perineum. If you've had a C-section, you're expected to be up and walking around mere hours after undergoing this major surgery where your intestines are moved outside your body and then replaced once the baby is removed. New babies wake every hour or so to feed or be changed and require constant care in a cycle that feels less like the "natural" experience it's touted to be and more like walking through a category 5 hurricane. You'd think that more men would step in to help their partners navigate this intense period of simultaneous healing and nonstop "care," but as we touched on briefly in chapter 2, in the UK, less than a third of men take their allocated two-week paternity leave, and only 60 percent of American men take theirs.[82] Why?

There's never just one answer to this kind of question, but a primary one is that many men are implicitly or explicitly discouraged from taking time off to support their partners and bond with their children, potentially because of career penalties and also because a man actively participating in a nurturing role is considered feminine and, therefore, weak.[83] The perpetuation of this "traditional" approach to parenting keeps women in cis-het relationships buried under the huge emotional and physical load of caring for a newborn. It also ensures that she remains the "expert" on the baby, who becomes her sole responsibility with dad relegated to the role of "babysitter" whenever he takes over to give her a break. And before anyone comes at us with the "biological" argument about the brain change that takes place in new mothers but not new fathers, allow us to blow your mind. A 2014 study by Ruth Feldman, professor of psychology and neuroscience at Bar-Ilan University in Israel, measured the brain activity of both heterosexual new moms and dads as well as homosexual dads.

While the brains of the heterosexual moms showed five times more activity in the emotion-processing region known as the amygdala, the brains of the heterosexual dads showed heightened activity only in cognitive circuits while the mom was around but activated the amygdala when she wasn't present. The brains of homosexual dads showed the same responses as both heterosexual moms and dads—i.e., activation of the emotional processing regions and the cognitive circuits.[84] So when someone trots out the tired trope of men's brains not reacting to children in the same way as women's, just know that it's a fallacy being perpetuated to keep men from actively engaging in nurturing roles and unpaid care work, something which has no value within the Patriarchy.

So how can a woman's mental load be decreased? The single best way is to share the load with your partner (we are going to assume for the below that you have one, but if not, substitute in whoever assists you on a daily basis), and that has to start in the home, particularly with how responsibilities are split and how boundaries are set:

How to Lighten Your (Mental) Load:

1. **Bring it to light.** You need to make your mental load visible to the other adults in your life, specifically your partner. Work together to create a chart or list that clearly states whose responsibility certain tasks are. Do not do work your partner is meant to do, as aggravating as it might be to see clothes piling up in laundry baskets or a sink filled with dirty dishes. You and your partner have an agreement to share these jobs, and you do not need more work. Try to be gracious with your partner if picking up this work is new to them, but do not take the work over for them.

2. **Take shared parental leave.** Uneven mental load becomes exacerbated if babies come into the equation. Women

should not be the sole baby expert in the house; ensure that both you and your partner learn how to soothe and care for your little ones. If your partner cannot take parental leave, then ensure that the mental load for the new baby is still being shared, even if that means you have to hide yourself away while the baby is inexpertly bathed, clothed, or fed. Practice makes perfect, and caring for children in a partnership means it's not just the woman's job to care for the kids.

3. **Be mindful.** Being rooted in the present moment is a skill that none of us are taught but is deeply important. This is particularly important if you have kids; both of you need to set aside time each day to be present. The more your children have to battle a phone or computer to get your attention, the more they will act out. Even negative attention from a parent is a win for a child who just wants your time. Be clear with your partner that they are in charge of the kid(s) when it's your turn to take a break. This will help prevent the inevitable "mom's in the bathtub, let's all join her" scenario.

4. **Ensure both partners are included.** This is particularly important when dealing with schools and healthcare providers. In the case of emergency numbers, should an illness or accident occur, make it clear that both partners are in charge of caring for your child and ask that a rota is used (i.e., if you called one partner about the last incident, call the other one this time). This ensures that both partners are involved fairly, and neither is exempted from parental duty. Also, when it comes to "parent engagement," where parents are asked to get involved with their children's school experience, it cannot just fall to mom to photograph the "traveling" stuffed animal or make sure homework is done on time. Statistically, children in a two-parent

household do better from a psychological, educational, and social perspective, not least because there will be increased resources (time, money, etc.) available for them.[85] We know this is not always possible, and we are in awe of the many single mothers making life work, no matter what, for the sake of their children. At the end of the day, if you're in a partnership, it's important to acknowledge that you both lead busy lives full of important tasks, but that your child(ren) is more important than anything work-related. If you can both stick to this approach, then you're on your way to a better-balanced partnership.

To learn more, please check out these additional resources:

Books

- Layne, Linda, Sharra Vostral, and Kate Boyer, eds *Feminist Technology*. Chicago: University of Illinois Press, 2010.
- Perez, Caroline Criado. *Invisible Women: Exposing Data Bias in a World Designed for Men*. London: Vintage, 2020.
- Traister, Rebecca. *Good and Mad: The Revolutionary Power of Women's Anger*. New York: Simon & Schuster, 2019.

Activists/ Influencers

- Aiko Mae *she/her*
  - Instagram @aiko.means.love
- Destini Ann
  - Instagram @destini.ann
  - TikTok @destini.ann
  - www.destiniann.com

- Destiny Bennett
  - Instagram @theycallmemamabennett
  - Tiktok @mamapapabennett
  - www.mamabennett.com
- Femislay *she/her/hers*
  - Instagram @femislay

CHAPTER 6
THE ONLY WOMAN IN THE BOARDROOM

The hardest times for me were not when people challenged what I said, but when I felt my voice was not heard.
                                                    –CAROL GILLIGAN

Lisa's Story:

When I started working in the construction industry, I was repeatedly asked by both men and women (in an incredulous tone) why I wanted to do this job. The implicit meaning of that question was: *why would a woman want to do a man's job?* It underlined the sentiment that met me every day on site: Men are expected here, so they are welcome. Women are not. I internalized that for many years and expressed it in my physical presentation. I kept my hair cut short, didn't paint my nails or wear much makeup, and certainly didn't wear noticeable lipstick. I wore collared work shirts, blazers, and slacks as if dressing like a man would make me appear more worthy of the job role I'd already earned through hard work. Every time I sat in a meeting, I carried all of this weight with me. I would sit in a room with men my age and older who could walk in and sit down without a second thought. How much more are you able to give to your *job and your team if you can just walk through the door and be yourself, unapologetically? Most of the men I worked with didn't have to work themselves up to feeling worthy of walking through the door and taking up space at the table. While I sincerely hope that there are women out there who don't feel all of this, I know it happens to most Black people, people of Color, disabled people, and people from LGBTQ+ communities on a daily basis. In my industry, I rarely see other women who do what I do; most of the women I come across work in design, financial, or administrative roles and if they sit in meetings with me, they do exactly what I used to do: they don't actively take up space at the table, they don't accept drinks (but they will make them), if they speak at all they do so quietly, and they begin most of their statements with an apology—"Sorry, but ...." All of this tells me that the job I do and the environment I work in is not a welcoming place for women, and a lot of that has to do with a certain feeling that tends to exist in a room full of men, which I call the "Boys' Club."*

The phenomenon of the Boys' Club crops up a lot when I speak to other working women. It's the pervasive, unspoken feeling that women are not welcome—in the boardroom, in certain parts of the office, or even in the company itself. That feeling can be communicated as simply as conversations stopping when a woman walks into a room full of men or past a group of men or when conversations loudly take place that do not involve or include anyone but the men speaking. One common example of this is when men speak about playing a sport, like golf, and arrange for "all of us" to play with the implicit understanding that the woman or women in the room are not invited. The belief is that "women don't play golf," so an invitation does not need to be extended to the entire room or group, which is also extremely limiting to disabled employees. One of the most damaging parts of this blatant exclusion is that when colleagues engage in activities external to the traditional workplace, a kinship is formed, and corporate forward-planning is commonly discussed. Both of these situations facilitate a man's ability to rise within a company, either through promotion or an evolving job role. When women are implicitly excluded from bonding events taking place outside of the normal working environment or normal working hours, their ability to create connections that aid on the path to promotion is cut short. The "Boys' Club" mentality also leaves women feeling like their voices aren't heard or valued in meetings.

As a project manager in the construction industry, I am nearly always the only woman in the boardroom. When I sit in meetings, I am surrounded by men, some of whom have a driving need to dominate the room and work hard to make me (and anyone else who doesn't fit in the traditional corporate paradigm) feel subordinate or cast doubt over what I say. This has been my daily reality for nearly two decades, so believe me when I say that, yes, this still happens. I have eyes on me from the minute I walk through the door: it's the probing scrutiny of the men in the room as they try to understand what my place is. Everything you do as a woman in a male-dominated environment is scrutinized. Every action and decision feels loaded with the invisible weight of societal expectation and the nuances that gendered power struggles bring with them. It was only in the last few years that I would take a central seat at the boardroom table. Previously, I would sit in a peripheral seat because I didn't know who else would be coming into the room and whether they'd be more senior than me. That thought would never occur to a man (I've polled many male colleagues about this). They enter a boardroom intrinsically knowing they are important enough to sit wherever they like. Just for the record, and this is as much for you as for my younger self: you need to take yourself seriously. Self-doubt shines like a beacon and can make you even more of a target. If you were invited to a meeting, sit wherever you want. You don't need to "earn" your seat.

There is a common misconception that the women in boardrooms are there because they are supremely confident in themselves and their skill set, but that's not always the truth. Most women who reach the boardroom do so through countless years of hard work that involves a lot of being taken for granted, a lot of being someone else's scapegoat, a huge amount of self-doubt, and far too much time battling office politics. So, when these women sit in the boardroom, they are surrounded by a cloud of historical emotional baggage that most men don't have. Women can read the complete works of Sheryl Sandberg and attempt to "lean in" every second of the workday, and we can force ourselves to take up space at the table, we can mimic aggressive behaviors typically associated with men in order to fight our way up the ladder. But it won't change that while this frenzied hustle takes place, being the only woman in the boardroom is stilll happening. Most men don't recognize it because it's their privilege not to, because boardrooms have historically been a male experience.

As we've said, most men walk into a boardroom and feel comfortable enough to take a seat wherever they like, ask for a drink, and start personal conversations with others. They are comfortable in this setting, but as women, that level of comfort is not typically our privilege. We are tentative when we choose our seats. We are not the loud voice at the tablesharing a story from our private life. We are the ones everyone looks at when someone mentions getting refreshments. Can there be a more polemic issue based on such a basic task? The seemingly innocuous act of hospitality that is often interpreted as a definitive gender marker which we have seen emphasized over and over again in the boardroom setting. While women view getting drinks for a group as being an active team member or a good host, men tend to view it as a servile task that's beneath them. There is a negative impact on women when they are helpful in the boardroom; they are perceived by their male counterparts as too easy-going and not "tough" enough to be a leader. Unfortunately, not being perceived as helpful is almost as bad as being seen as too helpful. A study at a company highlighted in the Harvard Business Review found that out of 200 reviews, women received feedback that they were "too aggressive" in 76 percent of the instances. In contrast, men only received this feedback in 24 percent of these instances.[86] Unsurprisingly, reviews of this kind can have a severe impact on career trajectory.

The experience of being invited to meetings only when you've achieved a senior level is not universal. In other industries, like tech, meetings can be excessive with far too many people invited. Adding to this, the culture of "meetings as progress" results in full workdays spent monotonously grouped together when the information could easily have been shared via email or saved for later down the road when there was actual progress to share. In these meetings, it can often be hard to get a word in edgewise or stand out in the crowd, especially if these meetings span multiple continents and departments. In these instances, stating your role or title early on and establishing your purpose for being there can eliminate uncomfortable situations where support responsibilities are incorrectly attributed to you. If you're feeling like your participation in a meeting is not required, querying what your intended role in the meeting is with the coordinator can help clarify what is expected of you and, potentially, give you a way out. Don't be afraid to question why you're attending a meeting or what is expected of you. It goes without saying that any queries you have should be put forward as professionally as possible, but sitting silently while your workday is wasted serves no one and certainly isn't a good use of company resources.

If you do experience being the only woman in the boardroom, we want you to know what it feels like so that when you're in there, suffering through the things we've described, you'll know that you're not the problem. If you're meant to be there, *know* that, no matter how uncomfortable you might be made to feel. When you enter a predominately male boardroom, you may worry about not having anything to say for the entire meeting or being made to look ridiculous. Many years ago, we were told that we had to be the person in the room who knows the answers to all the questions being asked. We have found that the only way to feel that level of confidence is to prepare for meetings comprehensively and well in advance. If you haven't adequately prepared for a meeting, you'll be on the back foot the entire time, which is deeply uncomfortable. One way to combat this is to do a checklist at the start of your day to understand what you expect yourself to achieve that day and cross off each task as you deal with it. Make sure you add on any new tasks you're given during the day; otherwise, you may get to the end of the day having accomplished nothing on your list and feel frustrated. Women are disproportionately given busy work (i.e., administrative tasks), and each workday can melt into the next. Keeping a daily list or record of what you've been given to do and what you've accomplished can help give you a better understanding of your actual workload.

Before important meetings, we like to follow the points on the following page to lay the groundwork. Some of these may seem like overkill for smaller meetings, and they may well be, but you only have to feel the sting of not having prepared enough once to appreciate that being over-prepared is much better than feeling completely lost.

How to Be a Fucking Rockstar (in the Boardroom):

1. **Know what the meeting is about.** We don't just mean knowing the subject: ensure that you understand what topics will be discussed in the meeting and, depending on what it is, have a basic grasp of the negative/positive impacts it is currently having on your project or team, what

obstacles it may present, and keep a list of any queries that come up for you while gathering information.

2. **Know the problems *and* the solutions.** Collate the information you collected in step 1 and streamline it into one list of objectives and one list of potential mitigation strategies. No one likes to be presented with a slew of problems and zero solutions; even if some of your solutions feel like "nonstarters," they will generate further discussion and potentially help lasting solutions emerge.

3. **Know the agenda.** If it's your meeting, you should issue an agenda at least twenty-four hours before the meeting takes place. This lets your attendees collect their thoughts and come prepared, which will, in turn, make the meeting a productive use of everyone's time. If it's not your meeting, request an agenda at least twenty-four hours before the meeting takes place if one hasn't been issued by that point.

4. **Know who will be attending.** This is obviously key if you're hosting the meeting, but if you're not the host, it's just as important for you to know who will be around the table. If there is someone on the invite list that you don't know, Google them so you can put a face to the name. This is a real must for new client meetings or initial project meetings. Knowing who people are around the table will not only give you confidence, it will display your preparedness.

5. **Know what your questions are.** Remember that list of queries you put together in step 1? Bring those to the meeting, and if they're not covered, you need to raise them. This will also help if you're struggling to find something pertinent to say during the meeting.

6. **Know what to take away.** Odds are there will be a handful of outstanding actions at the end of the meeting or points that need to be taken away and discussed. If it's your meeting, make sure you communicate this clearly to the

group and confirm who will own these actions. DO NOT take responsibility for actions that should not be yours, and do not hesitate to contradict anyone who attempts to give you deliverables that do not belong to you. Sloping shoulders are a common affliction, and women are raised to be people-pleasers—no one will reward you for doing someone else's job. You will only receive more of their work for none of their pay.

We spoke briefly about the fear of being too quiet in the boardroom, which is a pervasive feeling for many women in the corporate world. There are a slew of reasons behind why this happens, but one of the most insidious is that many women feel that they don't belong there and that they'll be "found out." For a long time, these feelings were defined as impostor syndrome, a term coined in 1978 by two White researchers, Dr. Pauline Clance and Dr. Suzanne Imes. What we know now is that the study wasn't based on a diverse set of of participants, and the impact of systemic racism, ableism, and other forms of discrimination weren't taken into account. This is a particular problem when we look at how Black women and women of Color are minoritized within the workplace. Using the term impostor syndrome erases, or at the very least minimizes, the impact of systemic racism and the many obstacles it represents in the corporate environment. Using impostor syndrome as a catch-all term for how women are made to feel in "traditional" workplaces puts the responsibility on their shoulders to fix, making systemic issues the fault of the individual woman. Feeling uncertain and anxious are almost universal, they affect everyone, but we do need to appreciate that the experience of women working in a male-centric environment is going to exacerbate those feelings. Just as Black women, women of Color, disabled women, and people from LGBTQ+ communities will feel heightened levels of anxiety, frustration, and self-doubt when they are faced with the obstacles placed in front of them within a workplace made by, and for, White cis-het, non-disabled men.

The old adage that "confidence is key" couldn't be more right, especially in the professional workforce. A 2002 survey of medical students on a surgery rotation showed that the women gave themselves lower scores than men even though their faculty consistently evaluated the women more positively.[87] A 2014 study of a wide swath of political candidates revealed that the male candidates were 60 percent more likely to say they were "very qualified" to run for office than the female candidates.[88] A 2019 working paper for the National Bureau of Economic Research found that women consistently rated their performance lower than men: while men gave themselves an average of 61 out of 100, women gave themselves an average score of 46. It's important to note that both groups had the same average score.[89] The research is even more staggering when it comes to promotion and salary: an internal report done by Hewlett-Packard found that female employees would only apply for a promotion when they met 100 percent of the job qualifications while men were confident enough to apply when they only met 60 percent of them.[90] Studies of business school students found that men initiate salary negotiations four times more often than women. When women attempt to negotiate their salaries, they ask for 30 percent less than their male counterparts.[91] What is going on?

There's both nature and nurture behind these behaviors, as scientists have discovered a few key differences between men and women. Women tend to activate their amygdalae, the brain's primitive fear center, more than men, which means we can form stronger, longer-lasting memories of our perceived failures. Some studies have suggested that women may have a larger anterior cingulate cortex, the part of the brain where we recognize errors and deliberate over options.[92] While current research tends to support that men's and women's brains are more similar than they are different, women still seem to revisit negative moments and torture ourselves over our past failings more readily while also allowing those incidents to impact our decision-making.

Could it be down to hormones? One of women's main hormones is estrogen, which encourages forming emotional bonds, making connections over causing conflict, and discourages risk-taking. Men also have estrogen, but their main hormone is testosterone, and in a study done by Forbes in 2018, they found that when people with higher levels of testosterone, which is associated with overconfidence and aggression, are given more access to power, they tend to become narcissistic and misuse their power.[93] Women have testosterone as well, but our typical levels are ten times less than men's. A research study at University College London (UCL) found that when women were given additional testosterone, they were wrong more often and struggled to collaborate,[94] so giving women more testosterone isn't the simple solution to increasing their confidence. It's important to note as well that in lab studies, animals with high levels of testosterone became so aggressive and overconfident that they often took fatal risks.[95]

We are not saying that all men are imbued with an overwhelming sense of confidence, but for the most part, it is not something they lack, and this helps them take risks and recover from failure, perceived or real, more quickly than women. Some researchers believe this stems back to early school years where boys tend to be more boisterous than girls and get into trouble more often for their struggle to sit still and listen, two things young girls tend to be good at. Many girls internalize the rewards that quiet, attentive behavior brings them, while boys receive punishment more often and learn to see failure as a normal part of life. Girls, and women, tend to see making mistakes and personal failure as a reflection on themselves, so many strive for perfection, and perfectionism is a confidence killer. Because of this, many women tend not to answer questions unless they know the answer is correct, they don't go for promotions unless they're 100 percent certain they're qualified, and they don't compete unless they feel confident they can win. In short, we focus all of our attention on trying to be perfect as employees, friends, partners, mothers, etc., which is a battle we can never win, and it's a serious roadblock to success. We hesitate to act at key points in our lives, and in doing so, we hold ourselves back; however, when we do force ourselves to act, women perform at the same level as their male colleagues, if not better.[96]

Unfortunately, telling women that confidence is as key to success as competence to spur them into action won't work for everyone. Women also pay the price for being too confident. We are often penalized both professionally and socially if we behave too confidently. Aggressive men conjure up the image of clever, hard-working executives while aggressive women are manipulators or "ball-busting bitches" (a term we first heard used by our father and then repeated during our professional careers). In a word, women who are perceived as being too confident are not likable. A study at the Yale School of Management found that when senior-level women spoke at work, both men and women found them less suited to being a leader than their male counterparts, even when they spoke the same amount. When senior-level women spoke less, they were perceived as more likable and competent.[97]

We know that women have all the skills necessary to excel in the corporate world. We tend to be acutely aware of threats, making us excellent strategists. Women typically score higher than men in having the five key leadership traits identified in a study by BI Norwegian Business School: emotional stability, extroversion, openness to new experiences, agreeableness, and conscientiousness. Women are excellent business owners because, even though they receive less than half the business investment that men get, they produce more than twice the revenue.[98] Several studies of hedge-fund managers have shown that investments run by female managers outperform those run by male managers.[99] Women's involvement in the corporate world is key for both their company and their country: the more diverse a company's leadership team is, the more innovative they are found to be,[100] and by closing gender gaps in the workplace and the wider world, we could potentially add $12 trillion to the global GDP within a ten-year span.[101]

We could go on because there are thousands of statistics to back up why women should be in every boardroom worldwide, *en masse*. Yet we also know that the work environment most women find themselves in is not conducive to excellence. So what can we do to change things?

Be *That* Bitch in the Boardroom (Tips to Empower Yourself):

1. **Sit at the table.** We're not just parroting Sheryl Sandberg here. You really do need to sit at the table, literally. Don't worry about who else might be coming into the boardroom, how many open seats are left, or whether you have the right to be there. If you were invited to the meeting, you're meant to be in the room. Own that and don't sit on the fringe, afraid to speak. Get dynamically involved in the conversation.

2. **Don't take any shit.** We don't care how long someone has been at a company or how much they get paid. They have not earned the right to demean anyone around the boardroom table (or anywhere else). If someone is talking over you, interrupting you, belittling you, or making you feel subordinate, then you need to call it out. You were hired to do a job. You were invited to a meeting to discharge your responsibilities. You have every right to confront someone not affording you the respect you deserve. If you're not sure if you're being treated unfairly, ask yourself if you've ever seen a man be treated the way you just were. That should make the answer clear pretty quickly.

3. **Only do YOUR job.** Companies tend to heap additional unpaid work and responsibilities on women because we don't like to say "no." Now is the time to learn the invaluable skill of NO: NO, you can't stay late to finish a report; NO, you can't make a round of drinks for a meeting; NO, you can't do admin work for your male colleague just because he's not "as good at it as you are." Make sure that you have an agreed roles and responsibilities document for your position (if you haven't done this, do it now!) and stick to that list. If your company asks you to do more than is on that list, then you need to be paid more to do it. It's as simple as that.

4. **Take it personally.** If someone at your company is rude, abusive, bullying, or making your work life difficult, report them. If you see or hear someone do it to someone else, report them, especially if others can't or won't do it for themselves. Record every instance of bad behavior when it happens—this can be a video, a picture, an email sent to your line manager or HR department, or a list of occurrences (try to include dates, times, and witnesses if you can). No one should be made to feel uncomfortable at work and, as intimidating as it can feel to report someone, just know that whatever you get "used to" will continue to happen and probably escalate. Protect yourself and others from future harm by holding people accountable for their bad behavior.

Regardless of how much you prepare, you may still have times at work where you feel out of place, nervous, scared to speak, dismissed, belittled, ashamed, or like you're a problem in some way. A large part of this is down to conditioning: from a very young age, many of us were told that we must be perfect, that failure is not an option, and that if we can't consistently excel, then we don't deserve a space at the table. It simply isn't true, and we need you to do everything in your power to combat that social conditioning and believe that you are meant to be there. You are worthy of and qualified for the job you hold, and you're a valid, important part of the team. The continual gaslighting and jockeying for position in the corporate world dovetails with our social conditioning and sets us up to doubt ourselves and yield ground to those who don't deserve it, forcing us to be hard on ourselves and on other women.

PLEASE learn to be kind to yourself and all of the women around you (not just the ones that look like you), trust your instincts, and work to build a community that builds women up and amplifies all women's voices. You are not in this fight alone, and other women are not your competition. There is plenty of space in the boardroom for all the women who want to be there.

To learn more, please check out these additional resources:

Books

- Bennett, Jessica. *Feminist Fight Club: An Office Survival Manual for a Sexist Workplace*. London: Portfolio Penguin, 2016.
- Brown, Brene. *Dare to Lead*. London: Vermillion, 2018.
- Scott, Kim. *Just Work*. New York: St. Martin's Press, 2021.

Activists/ Influencers

- Negotiation Tips & Strategies
  - Instagram @negotiatethis
  - www.negotiatethis.org/
- The Female Lead
  - Instagram @the_female_lead
  - www.TheFemaleLead.com
- Womenontopp.com
  - Instagram @womenontopp
  - www.womenontopp.com

CHAPTER 7
IS SISTERHOOD A MYTH?

I'm a feminist. I've been a female for a long time now.
It'd be stupid not to be on my own side.

–MAYA ANGELOU

There's a famous cartoon by Riana Duncan from the late '80s of a boardroom with six people in it, one woman and five men. The caption reads, "That's an excellent suggestion, Miss Triggs. Perhaps one of the men here would like to make it."[102]

It's both comforting and infuriating to know that this dismissive, sexist behavior has been happening for at least thirty years—comforting to know it's not just happening to us, infuriating that this has been commonplace for at least three decades and shows little sign of stopping.

In case you've never had this happen to you, let us just say that it is incredibly debasing to have a man repeat something you just said and watch the other men in the room agree with it or at least react to it, when it was either ignored or misunderstood when it came from you. It's the compounding of being obviously passed over in a room full of people and then watching a man steal your thunder and gather accolades that rightfully belong to you. It's a deeply diminishing experience, and it further underlines that your presence and voice as a woman are invalid in that space. This happens to women so often in the corporate world that there is a term for it: hepeating. And why "hepeat," you ask? Because the benefits for the men that do it are increased respect and esteem in the workplace including increased status such as promotion or leadership opportunities. The study that reviewed this phenomenon, published by the *Academy of Management Journal,* found that getting credit for ideas at work is something men do more than women. Men regularly experience the benefit of speaking up in meetings whereas women are consistently ignored, misheard, or misunderstood.[103] Hepeating is also done to Black men and women as well as men and women of Color;[104] it is yet another way in which the corporate world expresses its distaste for any derivation from the dominance of White men.

There are countless articles on the subject of hepeating, all of them confirming that it takes place but also placing the bulk of the responsibility for eliminating it squarely on women's shoulders. Advice typically ranges from being more assertive (i.e., speak louder!) so that your voice is heard, speaking more clearly, and presenting evidence to back up your statements. We came across the suggestion to try these options out on International Women's Day, which wrongly assumes that on that day our lady voices become stronger and more amplified. Another helpful article suggested increasing the number of women in the room to provide you with support, which we love the visual of: roaming the halls of your office with an entourage of girlfriends who have given up their plans for the day in order to back you up in work meetings because your male colleagues can't be bothered to pay attention to you when you speak. Iris Bohnet, a behavioral economist from Harvard, rightly calls hepeating a "microaggression," which is a subtle comment or action designed to negatively impact a person or group, and suggests micro-sponsorship, where you ask colleagues to advocate for you, to combat hepeating.[105] This is not our favorite suggestion as it doesn't attack the root of the problem; it simply shifts the voice asking for validation from female to male. Nothing is changing except you're now pandering to the Patriarchy by using a man's voice to ask for what should rightfully be yours. Bohnet also encourages women to be vigilant in ensuring that comments are attributed to their rightful originators,[106] something we do religiously no matter the setting. In the workplace, we see our female colleagues also regularly doing it, sometimes to their own detriment; however, only a handful of our male colleagues will do this in the office, much less in front of a client or external party. It should go without saying that this is something everyone should be doing. It takes nothing away from you to give your colleagues their kudos. In fact, it helps engender a strong sense of unity and might encourage others to follow suit.

If these strategies don't strike you as proactive enough, let's turn our eyes to Washington, DC, to see how women in this seat of heteropatriarchal (the intersection of cisgender heterosexuality and the Patriarchy) Western power make themselves heard. A 2016 article in the *Washington Post* by Juliet Eilperin discussed how the women on the White House staff, the author claims, came up with an effective rebuttal to hepeating that they call "amplification."[107] Amplification occurs when one woman in the boardroom makes a statement and the other women repeat what the first woman said, forcing recognition of it by the entire room. Don't you find it incredible that grown women are having to effectively hijack a meeting by onerously repeating what each of them says until it is heard and recognized by the men in the room? A few queries spring to mind:

- What do you do if there are no other women in the room?
- Why do women have to repeatedly parrot each other just to be heard?

- Why assume that all the women in the room work for the same company or are on each other's side?
- Further to the query above, are we to assume that all women belong to some sweeping, all-inclusive sisterhood?

The fourth question is the one that stirs us the most. We sincerely wish there was a unified sisterhood, backed by a universal playbook that all women had access to and that somehow managed to encapsulate our myriad experiences as women, no matter our race, sexual orientation, beliefs (both religious and cultural), and geographical location. It's hard to believe that such a thing could exist, and even if it did, its existence would be based on the assumption that all women consistently endeavor to act in the interest of both themselves and their sisterhood at all times.

If such a sisterhood did exist, what would its purpose be? The *Cambridge Dictionary* defines sisterhood as "a strong feeling of friendship and support among women who are involved in action to improve women's rights,"[108] which sounds pretty fantastic. Wouldn't it be wonderful to know that women around the world were committed to the creation and protection of such a powerful system?

Unfortunately, we don't all act in alignment with the definition of sisterhood. You only need to spend five minutes on any social media platform to see that. As we discussed in chapter 3, one of the principal actions of the Patriarchy is to keep women in a weakened state in order to oppress them, and this influence encourages women to view their sisters as competitors and enemies. We now do the work of the Patriarchy ourselves, especially when we use its demeaning and separating language. The Patriarchy demands that we reduce ourselves to objects to gain approval and offer up our sexuality in order to chase conditional and transitory admiration, so when a woman feels good enough about herself to post a selfie on social media, she will inevitably receive a slew of comments from other women lambasting her for being an attention seeker or a whore. The rise, or rather the definition and visibility, of the "pick me" has been meteoric. Women who belittle and distance themselves from other women in an attempt to insinuate themselves with men lean heavily into their own internalized misogyny, viewing expressions of femininity as an insult, and using the deeply damaged "I'm not like other girls" trope. This campaign of women against women has become more apparent and more recorded than ever thanks to the rise of social media—and in the corporate world, where so many women desperately need support, it rears its ugly head at every opportunity.

Having read through countless articles and studies on the effect the corporate world has on women, it's become apparent to us that most people place the onus on women to make changes in their own behavior in order to succeed instead of tackling the elephant in the room, i.e. the heteropatriarchal, systemically racist and ableist construct that the corporate world labors under. For example, many articles point to women taking things too personally at work as the main reason they cannot progress. Speaking to *The Telegraph*, career coach Corinne Mills said:

> *I definitely think women can take these things more personally. Most of the time, it's actually about getting things done and business decisions. But women invest emotionally in their job quite a lot, and their self-esteem is often linked to it. So, if what they think is a good idea isn't taken up, they can find it harder to not take it to heart. Generally, men can be more resilient and get on with the next plan of attack.*[109]

But haven't women been told for decades that the reason men can feel emasculated by women who make more than them is because their work is tied directly to their sense of self and, ultimately, their self-esteem? Men who get emotional about their work are committed, passionate, driven, ambitious. Women who do the same are reprimanded for taking it all "too seriously." The article goes on to say that women damage their career prospects when they overreact to competitive behavior in the office, like "power moves," which are actions and behaviors used to assert dominance and authority over colleagues.[110] Typical power moves used in office environments include purposely misspelling people's names, telling someone to do work that this person's higher-ups know he or she is already doing, ignoring people when they speak, or being the last one to show up for your own meeting. Women tend to see actions and behaviors like this, at best, as rude behavior—and at worst, as racist or sexist, and they are more likely to fall out with female colleagues whom they perceive to be acting this way. This does seem to speak to the existence of a belief by women, no matter how conflicted we are by the patriarchal conditioning that attempts to pit women against each other, that we shouldn't behave this way toward each other. A paper published by the *Journal of Personality and Social Psychology* detailed a series of tasks that women and men were asked to undertake while being told that a male and a female colleague were trying to outdo them and undermine their work. The study found that women who competed against each other found it "less desirable" than competing against their male colleagues. The men viewed competition against their female colleagues as "less acceptable" than competing against their male colleagues. It would appear women dislike competing against other women but seem to accept competing against men, which lends itself to the possibility that women actually do subscribe to the ideal of sisterhood. Men, on the other hand, dislike competing against women but seem to like to compete against each other.[111] Or do they?

If you believe the many articles written about competition among men in the corporate world, you'll come away thinking that men accept competition as a natural part of life and relish the challenges it brings. Except a lot of men actually don't. A survey of 15,000 employees by the UK health charity Mind found that one in three men blamed their work for negatively impacting their mental health.[112] A further study by the Men's Health Forum reported that 34 percent of men said they felt constantly stressed or under pressure and that they feared the reaction of their managers if they showed weakness or spoke about mental health problems. Men are also three times more likely to become alcohol dependent than women as well as more likely to use and die from illegal drugs, potentially using these as an ineffective and dangerous panacea for mental health issues.[113]

As much as our current social paradigm wants us to believe differently, excessive and prolonged competition in the workplace isn't good for anyone, and women aren't being too sensitive when they take it personally. It is personal to be pointedly ignored or maligned. It is personal to treat someone as "less than" to claim dominance over them, so we need to stop telling women that they are the ones who need to behave differently to succeed. And yet, when you look online, there has been a slew of "helpful" material published over the last decade telling women to change themselves in order to succeed in the corporate world. Here are some of the most hair-raising ones we came across:

- An article from the Stanford Graduate School of Business (March 2011) entitled "Researchers: How Women Can Succeed in the Workplace," which suggests that women who display masculine traits, but are able to turn them on/off, will get more promotions than men.[114]
- Monster.com's article entitled "Promotion Know-How for Women," which suggests that to be promoted, women need to do as much work as they can, as fast as possible, while also remaining happy and likeable.[115]

- An April 2014 article in *Forbes* entitled "The No.1 Way Women Can Succeed at Work," which starts with the memorable opening line of "Why are women sissies at work?" and goes on to chastise women for not talking enough and not taking enough credit.[116]
- The Daily Mail's 2012 article entitled "Women who want to succeed at work should shut up—while men who want the same should keep talking, research says" which pretty much says it all.[117]
- Last but not least, the advice of Katie Hopkins from 2014 in her column for *The Sun* where she stated that women should "use the power they have to get ahead" and "play the game of sex and power" by sleeping with their bosses.[118]

Women need to get "tougher," play the game, and stay even when they want to leave.[119] Mothers who work outside the home need to think like a chess master, planning for every eventuality, thinking of the long game, prepared to sacrifice pieces and ready to shift their idea of what "winning" actually looks like.[120] If this mishmash of guidance feels confusing, we couldn't agree more. There's no feasible way that women can act on all of this advice, not just because much of it is conflicting, but also because it still asks women (and men) to continuously assess and navigate the aggressive, toxic climate that many workplaces foster.

We need to acknowledge that the hypercompetitive nature encouraged in the corporate world is not sustainable, and career structures built upon this model are detrimental to people's mental, emotional, and physical health. Society is asking women to bow or bend to this model, which does not fit or suit them—though, in reality, it doesn't fit the men it was built for either. What is needed are workplaces that appreciate diverse skill sets and discourage backstabbing, petty office politics, and hypercompetitive behavior. These toxic behaviors are magnified within a setting that does not provide a level playing field to all and caps the number of leadership positions available. Women are being set up to compete in a way that exacerbates and magnifies every negative influence the Patriarchy has taught us to hold about other women.

An important patriarchal influence that we need to invesigate further is why we get jealous and envious of other women who succeed. Many of us were raised to be small, quiet, and humble. "Humble," in our opinion, is not what women should aspire to be: it's defined as not proud or believing that you're important,[121] all of which ties beautifully into what a "good woman" looks like through the lens of the Patriarchy. So when we, who have been painfully trained to be small, see other women living their lives loudly and beautifully, we hate them. We envy their success. We are jealous of their expansion, of seeing them claim the space that they, and we, deserve to occupy. We want to be able to do what they're doing. We all have a driving need to be our authentic selves, and when we see other women living their truth while we deny our own, there is a deep longing in us to do the same. Another woman succeeding doesn't mean that our ability to succeed is lessened. There is no quota for how many successful women can exist in the world at any one time. Just as there is infinite space for men to produce, succeed, and achieve, there is the same amount of space for all women to expand and become the most incredible versions of themselves in whatever capacity they are drawn to. When we understand and appreciate this space of expansive and infinite self-expression, it is easy to embody the mantra coined by Amy Poehler: "Good for her, not for me."[122] We can support and uplift our sisters, and ultimately the sisterhood, by understanding that the success of one woman is a thing of beauty, just as our success will be beautiful to our sisters.

So what can we do every day to engender success in our fellow women and promote sisterhood? Here are three simple things we work on every day.

Support Your Sisters (and Other Obvious Ways to Empower Women):

1. **Good for her, not for me.** Say it loud and say it proud. When you see another woman succeed, praise her for it. Tell her she is amazing, that you see the hard work she has done, that she deserves her success. If a little red flag pops up for you or something inside you twinges when you say it, find out what your inner self is trying to tell you. Your feelings of jealousy should be a call to action for you, not a call to get out the pitchforks. This needs to be our motto as women: "I am happy when another woman succeeds because it is beautiful and brings my own success that much closer."

2. **Stop talking shit.** We know, we know. It feels really cathartic to have a massive bitch session about someone who has made a very public mistake, received their perceived comeuppance, or been brought "down to size." Gossip has been associated with women for eons, mainly because most of us like to "talk it out" as a way to relieve stress and connect, and it is a natural progression in a vent session to get personal about someone else, but we have to stop doing this. We have to stop running down other women to gain power for ourselves, whether that power comes from feeling righteous, superior, or dominant in some way. We should not be fighting over crumbs from the table; we need to sit down at the table ourselves. Garner more power for your life through positive action, not through denigrating and demeaning other women. All of us have enough battles to fight without turning our hearts against each other.

3. **Unlearn your hate.** Babe, you've absorbed a lot of bad habits. You've been taught to look for love and acceptance externally. You've been taught to drown your pain with chemical substances. You've been taught to starve yourself

for beauty, and you've been taught that youth is god. You're smart enough to know all of it is a lie, but you need to recognize that you're holding onto these lies before you can do the work to remove them from the foundation of who you are as a woman. If you want to become the best possible version of yourself, then this is necessary work, not just to strengthen the woman in you but to accept and support the women around you. Do the work. We promise that you won't regret it.

To learn more, please check out these additional resources:

Books

- Adegoke, Yomi, and Elizabeth Uviebinené, eds. *Loud Black Girls: 20 Black Women Writers Ask: What's Next?* London: 4th Estate, 2021.
- Fujiwara, Lynn and Shireen Roshanravan, eds. *Asian American Feminisms and Women of Color Politics*. Seattle: University of Washington Press, 2018.
- Lorde, Audre. *When I Dare to be Powerful*. London: Penguin Books, 2020.

Activists/ Influencers

- Adrienne Maree Brown (she/they)
  - Instagram @adriennemareebrown
  - www.adriennemareebrown.net
- The Boss Collective
  - Instagram @theboss_collective

CHAPTER 8
THE PENALTY FOR LEANING OUT

Each time a woman stands up for herself, without knowing it, possibly without claiming it, she stands up for all women.
                                                        —MAYA ANGELOU

Lisa's Story:

Female project managers in the construction industry are thin on the ground, so we're a valuable commodity to exploit. I used to imagine myself as one of the world's last white rhinos being put on public display each time I got trotted out at project interviews in order to show prospective clients that my company was "progressive" because it had hired a woman to do a role traditionally done by men. I would sit in the interview and listen to clients being told that I was the head of construction for my business unit, or that I was a senior project manager, long before any of that was true. When I spoke, I could tell that my words had more weight because of my trumped-up title. Those titles stayed behind when I left the room and went back to being just another project manager among my male colleagues. The difference was that, given enough time and effort on their part, my male colleagues probably would become senior project managers and heads of construction while I'd never seen women hold those roles. None of my managers were particularly smart or savvy, but they all tended to know a little bit about building, a little bit about problem-solving, and could speak confidently to clients. They were also all men; I have never had a female boss, nor have I worked in a company with a woman in a senior operations position. In 2018, a survey by Randstad (a recruitment agency) reported that more than half (52 percent) of the women they interviewed had never had a female manager,[123] so what I've experienced isn't an anomaly. It's also not a one-off that, for many years, I got paid significantly less than my male counterparts, even though my work has always been highly regarded. How else would I have lasted in an industry where, as with most male-dominated industries, women have to be twice as good as their male counterparts in order to be recognized as equal? Construction, like so many industries, has shielded the truth of its inequitable pay structure by allowing a culture of fear around discussing income to pervade the industry. Because openly discussing how much you earn is generally regarded as rude in the UK, it was accepted practice at most of the firms I worked for that you weren't allowed to talk about your salary. At the first construction company I worked for, discussing your pay with another employee was a fireable offense. To try and get employees to toe that line now would go down like a flaming brick, but a decade and a half ago, inculcating a culture of fear was standard practice. Some of this culture of fear still exists and is an important reason behind why women can find it so frustrating to work in a male-dominated profession. When we encounter misogyny, racism, harassment, or bullying in the workplace, the consistent message is that nothing will change because every construction company out there has the same "problems"—so shut up and deal with it, or you'll be fired.

When speaking to female colleagues about issues they have at work, the most consistent comment I hear is, "What's the point *of leaving when every other company is exactly the same?" It's a creeping and poisonous feeling of complacency that seems to increase in direct correlation with continued exposure to inequity. For example, some of my female work colleagues were talking about one of our company directors on a recent night out, a man who was notorious for doing very little actual work. His workday consisted of walking around the office chatting, holding pointless meetings with suppliers, which tied up meeting rooms for hours, and continuously stirring the pot of office politics. He didn't start his workday early, leave late, work weekends, or put in any of the extra effort that my female colleagues were consistently doing. Imagine their surprise when this director mistakenly sent an email to the entire company with a document attached showing his annual salary, which was extortionate. My colleagues were under no illusion that his pay would be in the same range as theirs, but they didn't expect it to be so grossly inflated that all their salaries combined couldn't touch it. Not only that, they could see that the company was paying for him to have private health care, something we had all been told was not an option. They were justifiably outraged, but when I asked what they planned to do about it, every single one of them said that they didn't feel there was anything they could do. They were more afraid of what would happen to their professional trajectory at the company if they raised it rather than addressing the clear imbalance that was taking place. So the situation continues: this hugely overpaid director works a six- to seven-hour day while they all regularly work ten- to twelve-hour days in the fruitless hope that someone will see their hard work and validate their effort with a raise or promotion. How can this be right? How can this be the result of the hard work, dedication, and drive to achieve that most women exhibit and all companies say they so badly need?*

Working women, especially those in male-dominated industries, tend to become complacent with, and accept, the status quo—not because we want to, but because we are bombarded with it every minute of the day. We get the overwhelming feeling that men, usually White men, have always been the boss and earned astronomically more than women. We can't achieve the same career heights, no matter how hard we work. Because of this, many of us accept what we're given because we feel like it's the best we'll ever get; some women even feel like someone did them a favor just for hiring them. "It's so frustrating to see women feeling this way, especially when we know that women tend to work 10 percent harder than men, not (just) because they're incredible workers, but because they are given, on average, 10 percent more work to complete than men. This work is usually administrative or "busy work," the time-consuming paper shuffling that keeps companies running but never leads to a promotion for the person getting it done.[124] So, if a man and a woman work from 9:00 a.m. to 5:00 p.m., then the man can stop work at 4:12 while the woman continues to work right up until 5:00. What would you do with that spare forty-eight minutes if you had it? Go get a manicure or a massage; meet up with a friend; dismantle the Patriarchy?

When we succumb to complacency, we become our own worst enemies. Women tend to be perceptive; we quickly grasp when situations are unfair, and perhaps because we're used to it, we have an instinct for picking up on inequality. Maybe you work at a company where it is implicitly understood and accepted that the pay ratio between men and women is imbalanced or where women are constantly surrounded by behavior that is racist, sexist, or discriminatory in some way. You might know that you're not happy or that you don't like some of the behaviors you regularly see or situations you find yourself in, but you don't say anything because you feel like complaining isn't allowed. In the corporate world, women are regularly marginalized, objectified, silenced, undervalued, or seen as niche commodities and bargaining chips. We know this isn't right, but because we've been told that "this is just how things are" and that it won't work out well for us if we cause "trouble," we keep our heads below the parapet and let ourselves become subordinate. It gets ingrained in our psyches that our collective suffering, our negative experiences of working in the corporate world are just part of existing as a woman in this world. As unfair a burden as it is to bear, accepting that reality is a key reason behind why it still exists. While we are loath to give women any further work to do to make their own lives fair, especially Black women and women of Color who are continually under attack, a sweeping change has to take place in order for all of us to feel like equality is worth fighting for and what we deserve.

The strongest position to negotiate from is when you don't *need* whatever it is you want to negotiate. When you sit around a table with people who want you more than you want them, there is a very clear distribution of power in your favor. So often as women, we find ourselves in positions of desperation where we're begging for a promotion, begging for a job, begging to be seen and validated. When we're begging for something, we're *asking* for it, not informing someone that it is what we *require*. When people think we're asking for something, it makes what we're asking for an option—and it is much easier for the person sitting across the table to say "no" to us than when that person is being told, "This is what I need in order to continue with you."

If you're working for a company that doesn't value you, you will have no power to negotiate. Let's put aside the obvious fact that you shouldn't be working anywhere that doesn't value you, because we know *you* know that. What you might still say, however, is that there aren't many job options near you, or that your life is complicated and the job you have allows your life to work, or maybe you want to switch careers but first you need to save money. All those excuses can be true for you, until they aren't anymore. If that sounds harsh, please hear us out.

If you've listened to our podcast, you'll know that Lisa said for a very long time that she didn't want to leave her job (where she was not respected or valued) because her life was complicated, because she didn't know if she still wanted to do the job she was doing, and because her job, which sucked, nonetheless allowed her to (sort of) balance her life. The day Lisa decided that she wanted to leave, that she had put enough money aside to take a break, catch her breath, and look around, was a transformative day. It was the day that she could, and did, say to her boss, "I need a break, and if you can't give me one, I'll have to quit."

Her boss spoke to his boss, and they agreed to give her a break. While she was on her break, other companies asked if she would come talk to them, and she did, but because she didn't need another job, she went in as her full self with no expectations. Lisa spoke in every interview about her son, her need for flexibility, and her commitment to her personal life. She let absolutely every person she encountered know what her requirements were to even consider taking a new job. Some of the companies fell away; some of the companies remained interested; but absolutely every company knew exactly who Lisa was (and is): a mother who chose to work outside the home, who was committed to her family, and who would not be fucked around.

Some of you might say, big deal, every mother who works outside the home talks about her kids, and every woman talks about her personal responsibilities at work. That may be true for some women, but for us, especially for Lisa, this was not the case. She had spent every day of the last five years since her son was born apologizing for getting to work "late," for taking personal calls at work, for leaving "early," for having to work from home because her son was sick or school was closed. Her entire working life was one big apology for daring to have a personal life in addition to a professional one, and every company Lisa worked for ate up her sacrifice and asked for more. These companies—which had promised her work-life balance and flexible working at the interview stage—chewed her up, spit her out, and left her with the constant feeling of being a failure. She would work harder for longer, never turn her phone off, answer every email regardless of the time. Her personal life faded into the background of a job that didn't fulfill, excite, or inspire her. Now maybe that was the job itself, or maybe it was the unceasing pressure of doing her absolute best and coming up short every time. Whatever the reason, the day that Lisa chose to step back and re-center her life around herself and her family with her work as the satellite, instead of the other way around, was the day that she empowered herself to do better and achieve more.

For all the mothers who work outside the home: you do not have to leave your family life at the office door. For way too long, the advice has been to work like you don't have a family, then raise a family like you don't have a job. This approach doesn't work—you cannot make it work, at least not long-term. If you're a mother who works in the corporate world, *own* your family. *Own* the fact that you need to work flexible hours to make your work-life balance actually happen. *Own* the fact that you have kids. *Own* the fact that you are a woman who, despite already working the equivalent of two and a half full-time jobs as a mother,[125] actively chooses every day to have *another* full-time job. And you're such a badass that you can do both, and everyone will survive, as long as there is balance and respect. You can take conference calls in your car on the way to watch your kid's school play, and if a family member gets sick or needs your support, the universe will not implode. Your company, your team, your work: they'll all survive you stepping away to care for yourself and your loved ones, and when you come back, you'll be more than ready to handle any of the dramatic minutiae that might have arisen while you attended to your number one priority—your personal life.

We are sick and tired of women being hung out to dry by literally everyone (even other women, the gasp, shock, horror of it all) because they have chosen to have a family *and* a career. Just as it's okay *not* to have children and okay to stay home with children if you decide to have them, it's also perfectly okay to want something else outside of eighteen-plus years of unmitigated, concentrated motherhood. Wanting more doesn't make you a selfish, uncaring, bad mother. What's *not* okay is for the patriarchal structures of the corporate world to vilify and condemn women instead of supporting them.

The corporate world has beaten so many people into believing that they're lucky even to have a job, that people will accept any kind of abusive behavior under the guise of "that's just the way it is." It doesn't have to be that way anymore. Women: do not accept any job offer that does not offer you the flexibility you need to make your life work—but more importantly, do not entertain any job offers from companies that show themselves to be unwilling to find a compromise. If you're chasing a dream job and you have to jump through a million fiery hoops just to be considered, do not expect a soft landing when you fall. That company is already not recognizing and honoring your humanity. It will not look kindly on your need to maintain a healthy work-life balance. It will not be a company that allows you time and space to heal from the inevitable grief or struggle we all face at some point during our working lifetimes. This is not the place for you. Find the place that actively seeks you out. A place that introduces you to different levels of managers who don't shy away from questions about flexibility and caring responsibilities. A place that recognizes the importance of *your* mental health.

No breakthrough moments are ever originally considered a viable option. When you ask for something different for yourself, it won't feel comfortable. It will feel like you are asking for more than you are owed or making excessive demands, and there is little doubt that whoever you initially approach about these issues will make sure that you walk away feeling like that. But what benefit do we get by not speaking up—job security at a company that treats you like shit anyway? Also, what happens when younger women come into the business and watch these injustices happen on a daily basis with no one fighting against them? We become an accomplice to the normalization of discriminatory behavior. We get blood on our hands as well. A common fallback is to locate a male "savior," a man who will amplify your own voice, but that isn't what's needed. All women have voices; if they're not being heard, it's because they're being actively silenced. Having a male colleague amplify the words you are trying to say doesn't fix the issue. You will still be a woman who isn't being heard. We have to take back the authority and influence that has been stripped from us, but how can we do that, especially if we've never been shown how? Four words: step into your power.

This phrase, which has been bandied about for years, has a multitude of meanings and definitions, all of which boil down to one simple thing: embrace the awesomeness that is you. Here are a few great definitions that resonated with us:

- To be in your power is to claim your joy, deliver your gifts, and own your part in the life you create.[126]
- Recognize and accept that you are complete within yourself, without the need for any particular thing, person, circumstance, or outcome. Give up the illusion that anything outside of yourself gives you happiness, control, or power.
- Be courageous enough to listen to your heart. To ask for what you want. To speak up and speak out. To say yes to the life you really, truly want. To do the thing you thought that you couldn't, and do it authentically and audaciously.

If you're a woman who has been continually made to feel powerless, voiceless (or silenced), or subordinate, then your focus needs to be on generating power within yourself in order to turn up your volume and make yourself heard. Some women already know how to generate their own power, but others might not know where to start. If that's you, we'd like you to ....

Initiate Empowerment Sequence:

1. **Understand who you are.** This is not a five-minute activity, nor is it static: who you are as a woman can, and should, change as you mature and your life evolves. Learning who we are as women and what we value is a lifelong journey, one that we have to regularly engage in order to understand our key motivators and how we draw our boundary lines.

2. **Recognize what your strengths are.** You don't need to be good at everything. Oprah spoke about how in her early TV career she thought she needed to do everything, and so she did, poorly. She quickly realized that she had to focus on what she did well, which was bringing knowledge and building a spiritually empowering movement and left the rest—booking guests and organizing the show—to her team.[127] Focus on what absorbs and activates you. Your passions will inevitably lead you to what you're good at, and when you hone in on them, make an effort to educate yourself as much as possible. That doesn't need to be a postgraduate degree or two years of night school. It can be a deep dive into books or podcasts on your chosen subject by thought leaders in the field. Arm yourself with as much knowledge as possible.

3. **Look to the future.** Where do you see yourself in two years, five years, ten years? Are there women in those positions already? If so, contact them and try to engage their help so that you can learn from them, potentially as a mentor.

Mentors ensure the transmission of knowledge to others, assist in the development of a competent workforce, and provide a mechanism for organizational learning,[128] so having this kind of insider knowledge on your side would be an incredible benefit. If you don't see any women in those roles, we suggest you reach out to the men in those positions as you would a woman and ask for advice. Be forewarned that you may struggle due to men in senior positions tending to be cautious about engaging in mentorships with women because of the way it "looks." A 2010 study from the Center for Talent Innovation found that nearly two-thirds of male executives pulled back from one-on-one contact with junior female employees because of the fear of being suspected of having an affair while half of junior women reported being nervous about one-on-one contact with senior men for the same reason.[129] As we said in chapter 2, it's #notallmen, but if you don't feel 100 percent comfortable with it, then revert back to point #2 and educate yourself as much as you can, in any way that you can.

4. **Make regular self-care nonnegotiable.** It's way too easy to put the things that help you relax, de-stress, and cut off on the back burner. We know that you lead a busy life and have a lot on your plate. That means you need self-care even more. There will never be a time when regular self-care is not a requirement for being the best version of yourself; the harder and more hectic your life gets, the more you need to find a safe space that nourishes you and allows you to shut up shop, even if it's only for thirty minutes. Meditate, get a massage, get your hair done, take a ceramics class, or go dancing, swimming, fell walking, whatever. All of it counts as self-care if you're cutting off from work and whatever personal responsibilities you have in order to focus on yourself.

Self-care is a pivotal part of managing our work-life balance. We've all seen enough Sheryl Sandberg TED talks to know that we are expected to lean in, overextend, and support every pillar in our lives with the same gusto and ambition that we had as single women in our early twenties. But it isn't possible to consistently sustain that level of energy, especially if you have a family or personal circumstances that put restrictions on your available time. Also, at what point did working forty hours a week turn into a part-time job? There is an expectation now that we all be work-accessible ninety-plus hours a week. You work all day with no definable break; eat lunch hunched over your desk; your work phone stays on all night and over the weekend; when you answer emails at 2:00 a.m. you're congratulated for your dedication. All this while companies loudly proclaim that they promote a healthy work-life balance for their employees when nothing could be less balanced than meeting these kinds of unspoken requirements. It is not sustainable, and if you try to conform to this frenzied work-life "imbalance," you will burn out, and it won't just be at work, but at home as well. When the workload for your paying job is heavy, stress levels rocket, and that doesn't stay in the office; it comes home to roost. We have no patience with our partners or our kids (if we have them), we're too busy or tired to connect with friends, and ultimately, everything in our lives suffers when we have too much on our plates.

How can we possibly make this new reality work when we as women are expected to work the same extended workday as our male colleagues yet still be responsible for the majority of the household chores and take up the mantle of the primary caregiver for our children? If you have children, you'll know it's a job that runs twenty-four hours a day, seven days a week, for (at least) eighteen years. The answer is that you can't do both, or rather, you can't do both well. If you try to juggle both a career and family life, you will find that either your home life is suffering, or you're being left behind when it comes to promotions and new opportunities.

Even if you can find some kind of balance in the two, you will still spend a great deal of time feeling like you've failed in some respect. There will always be some burning reminder that no matter how under control you feel like you have things, you're not actually winning, you're just surviving.

As if that wasn't enough, if you're a mother who also works outside the home, you're working harder and getting paid less than not just men, but also your female colleagues who don't have children. Mothers who also work outside the home in the US earn $16,000 less a year on average than working women without children,[130] and in the UK, a mother who also works outside the home can earn as much as 45 percent less than non-mothers.[131] It's called, unsurprisingly, the motherhood penalty, and it's a measure of the pay gap between mothers and non-mothers (women without dependent children) as well as mothers and fathers.[132] It's different from the gender pay gap, which is a measure of the pay gap between all working women and men; if you're a mother who also chooses to work outside the home, you're effectively penalized twice within the corporate setting. All the studies that have been done on the motherhood penalty show that women experience a fall in pay when they have a child and that the "penalty" rises with each period of maternity leave they take.[133] In a cis-het partnership, the income of the father is not negatively impacted by childbirth; in fact, a study by the Trades Union Congress (TUC) showed working fathers earning as much as 22 percent more than men without children.[134] There are many reasons why this pay gap exists, but the key issue is the inability of most working mothers to work long hours or respond to last-minute work demands (also the reason why many mothers work part-time jobs, earning less on average and increasing the gender pay gap) contrasting with the ability of fathers, men, and women without unpaid care responsibilities to commit to longer working hours. This is often interpreted as better work performance and greater dedication, garnering higher income for fathers, men, and women without dependents.[135]

We know that motherhood is not a choice that all women make; however, for those who do, there should not be a significant penalty levied against those who leave the workforce to start a family and then want to reenter it. Studies have shown that this phenomenon cannot be fully explained statistically which strongly suggests that cultural factors, like what society deems appropriate behavior for women who become mothers, are at play here. The corporate world tends to take a dim view of women who have children and want to work because it doubts the commitment of a working mother, yet it never doubts the commitment of a man who has children, in fact working fathers tend to be celebrated for their dedication to earning more for the sake of their families. When a woman attempts to do the same thing, she's heavily scrutinized.[136] Or perhaps it is part of the larger cultural expectation of what is expected of a mother: stay home and devote the rest of your adult life to your children once you have them, which is something we simply cannot accept. Just like we cannot accept any situation where a woman is being dictated to by a person or entity that has no understanding of their situation. Only you know what is right for your life, and if that means needing to take a step back, then so be it.

Sometimes you have to choose to lean out before you burn out and accept the penalty of taking back control. Part of that is knowing who you are as a woman and what you truly need to live your best life, but another integral part of it is self-care. Choosing not to be a doormat is a big decision and one that a lot of women have yet to make. We know that social media shows you the perfect version of women leading phenomenally perfect lives, but we need you to let that go and embrace the good-enough life. Be the good-enough employee, the good-enough partner, the good-enough mother. Be the good-enough version of you as a woman, and you just might surprise yourself when you find that a good-enough life ends up being way more fulfilling than constantly chasing the hollow dream of perfection.

If your knee-jerk reaction is that you don't want "good enough," you want something extraordinary, believe us when we say that we do too. We want to fly the flag of success from every pole, shout for equity from the rooftops, and encourage women to pursue their ambitions in the largest arenas. What we are talking about here is shirking the bite-sized vision of success that our mothers and grandmothers dared to dream and handed down to us. We reject the idea of success that only fills a man-shaped hole; we do not accept "having it all" in the boring ways the world has formerly permitted us to.

If you're struggling to forge your own "good enough" path, then the guidance by Marissa Orr to *Forbes* might resonate with you. Orr is a former Google and Facebook employee and author of *Leaning Out*,[137] a book about how corporate dysfunction is the reason for the gender pay gap, not women's lack of ambition and ability. We've reinterpreted Orr's favourite tips for leaving behind the success myths of the corporate world and included them below.

Leaning Back (Not Letting Go):

1. **Redefine what success looks like.** How you feel needs to be just as important as what you're achieving. It's great when you're winning, but if you feel like shit while you're doing it, the shine wears off pretty quickly. Choose goals that allow you to maintain a healthy life balance while consciously directing your own career trajectory. Don't blindly accept someone else's idea of what success is.
2. **Make your life about YOU.** Are you doing what you love or what your parents, family, friends, etc. want or expect you to

do? Every element of your life should reflect what's important to you, not what you've been told should be important.

3. **Know thyself.** How can you know what you want and need from a career if you don't truly know yourself? Take the time to get to know who you are, what inspires you, and what matters to you so that you have the framework for a future that will fit you and, hopefully, evolve with you over the years to come.

4. **Every company will have limitations.** No job can fulfill every single one of your career ambitions; it's simply not possible. Your work life needs to be a balance of what you bring to a company and what they bring to you. It's like any relationship: if you depend on one person to fulfill all your needs, you'll always be let down. Know that all of your career ambitions might not be met by the company you work for, and that's okay. That being said, your relationship should not be an abusive one. Both you and your company should be bringing your best selves to the table and showing each other the respect you deserve.

5. **The forty-year test.** Will what you're worrying about matter in forty years' time? Will it be something you still regret doing/not doing, or will you have forgotten it? This is a great question to apply not just to big decisions like moving jobs (or countries), but also as a measuring stick for what you should be spending your emotional energy on. Chances are that "future you" might be supremely unbothered by some of the things ruffling your feathers on a daily basis.

6. **Don't forget your journey.** Do NOT take career (or life) advice that doesn't dovetail with your own lived experience. Nothing in life is "one size fits all," and that is especially true of career success. What happened in your past has molded who you are as a person. Let your story help guide you to what's next.[138]

Whatever you ultimately choose to do in your career, whether that's to lean out, lean in, or stay the course, it needs to be the right choice for *you* first. For women, the word "selfish" is often used in response to any action we might take that doesn't consider everyone else before it considers us. Leave that bullshit behind. It will only see you working at a job you don't love, dreading the workweek, and effectively wishing your life away while you dream of early retirement. Don't be the woman who regrets any more of her wasted time; make the choices now to engender a life that fulfills you. You deserve it.

To learn more, please check out these additional resources:

Books

- Kinser, Amber E. *Motherhood and Feminism*. Berkeley, California: Seal Press, 2010.
- Selvaratnam, Tanya. *The Big Lie: Motherhood, Feminism, and the Reality of the Biological Clock*. New York: Prometheus Books, 2014.

Activists/ Influencers

- Mother Honestly
  - Instagram @motherhonestly
  - www.motherhonestly.com
- Seramount
  - Facebook @seramount
  - www.seramount.com
- Totum Women
  - Instagram @totumwomen
  - www.totumwomen.com

CHAPTER 9
KISSING THE EXECUTIONER

Women belong in all places where decisions are being made.
It shouldn't be that women are the exception.
—RUTH BADER GINSBERG

Jenni's Story:

We've all been there: sitting in a meeting, hands trembling, cheeks flushed, maybe a lump in your throat making it hard to speak or swallow. Filled with rage or frustration, tears threatening to well in your eyes, knowing you should say something, but you just can't make the words come out. Maybe you laugh uncomfortably, even though there is nothing funny about what is happening to you. You're face-to-face with men saying inappropriate things to you or around you, speaking over you, insinuating things about you in a "joking" way, or just generally behaving inappropriately.

What are your options in this situation? If you don't say anything, you're enabling bad behavior and, ultimately, helping to perpetuate a degrading, sexist culture in your company. On the other hand, it's terrifying to speak out, and it shouldn't fall to those being bullied to eradicate the bullying behavior on their own. We *can't allow people to openly abuse us or our coworkers, but if the thought of speaking up terrifies you, just know that you're not alone. I'm very familiar with the painful paralysis that strikes in these situations: knowing that you should say something, that it's time to speak up for yourself or a colleague, but you're physically unable to do so because you fear for your job or don't feel strong enough to take on the person who is being inappropriate. There have been many times in the past that I wished I had spoken up when I was insulted, humiliated, or demeaned in meetings, at business dinners, or social gatherings with coworkers.*

Early in my career, I was at a business dinner where I was the only woman. I was quite young and working in finance at the time. The men at the table talked about golf, and wanting to be an active participant, I said, "I really need to pick up golf." One of the men turned to me and said, "No, you should be at home with a husband making babies," and every man at the table looked at me and laughed. I laughed too because I felt like I had to, but I simmered with the shame of letting that man silence and belittle me. I should have said something, but I didn't feel strong enough to have that conversation yet, though being older and having more experience don't always mean that a woman is ready to be confrontational.

At the 2019 Tiburon CEO Summit the keynote speaker compared securing a client to getting into a woman's pants before taking the analogy even further.[139] After the story took off, two female CEOs who attended the talk were interviewed, and both of them confirmed that it had happened and that they had sat there stunned, thinking, "Is this really happening?" While I'm sympathetic to a point, most women can tell if they're in a room with the kind of man who speaks and behaves like this. We develop a sort of radar for it especially if we've worked in the corporate world. I'm willing to bet that both of those women knew pretty early on that, at some point, this man was going to be offensive in a way that would alienate them even further in a room where they were already the minority. The thing that struck me wasn't that a man felt comfortable to speak publicly in this way, because, honestly, it's still commonplace despite corporate PR trying to convince us that this kind of thing is dying out. Here's what I couldn't get past: the two female CEOs weren't the ones to speak out about this situation. It took a male journalist breaking a nondisclosure agreement (NDA) to bring this instance to light. I'm assuming that the two female CEOs are powerful, smart, and strong; a woman has to possess those characteristics (and a lot more) to reach the level of CEO. Even so, they were silent in a moment when they should have either spoken up or walked out. By sitting there, stunned, they gave up their power to this man because that is what a woman's silence does in moments like these. If a woman has broken into the rarefied executive atmosphere, she should feel a duty to use her amplified voice to help the women below and around her, but many women don't feel that they have the power to do so, despite their senior positions. That's because speaking out about sexism in the workplace puts a target on your back, something I know all too well.

I had a coworker who, during a presentation, said, "What we are dealing with are throwaways, like apple pie and motherhood." I had never heard that idiom before and certainly had never heard anyone refer to motherhood as a throwaway. What does that even mean? I immediately asked my coworker to repeat his statement and explain his intended meaning, while everyone else in the room just shook their heads and laughed. In the past, I would never have done something so "feminist" as to stand up for motherhood, but I could not let it slide like every other person in the room seemed able to. As my coworker bumbled through a response, I inwardly seethed. For a man to boldly term motherhood as a throwaway was to actively undermine everything that I, as a working mother, embodied. It somehow seemed to simultaneously amplify and diminish my recent struggles with working while pregnant, navigating maternity leave, and assimilating back into the workforce after nearly a year away caring for my new baby. He was implicitly telling me that a woman's place was in the home, working at an unpaid job that carried no weight in the wider world, much less the corporate world. It underlined the impossible expectations women face if they return to paid work after having a baby: work like you don't have a family, and mother like you don't have a (paid) job. His statement felt immensely disrespectful to me, and yet he was totally oblivious to the weight and impact of his words.

By asking him to repeat himself and explain the meaning of his statement, which he couldn't coherently do, I made many people in that meeting room uncomfortable, myself included. I was relatively new to the company, and this man was many times my senior, making three to four times my salary, and I had publicly called him out for what felt like sexist behavior. We finished the meeting after our "showdown," and he privately apologized to me, though that wasn't the first offensive thing I had heard him say, nor would it be the last. Later that year, he was quietly let go, ostensibly for other reasons, but I know I wasn't the only person to complain about him, though I was the only one who had openly challenged it. I was treated differently after that day in the boardroom; I was a troublemaker now, no matter how hard I worked or how many advances my project team and I achieved. I was never given the proper credit for my work, and my accomplishments were not lauded within the company like those of my male colleagues. I was the squeaky wheel because I would not tolerate bad behavior, and even though it led to me being ostracized within the company, I still felt empowered by using my voice.

I know women who work for companies that support them, have helped them hone their skill sets, and are respected and applauded for their efforts in the fight for gender equity. In general, though, speaking out at work in defense of yourself or your colleagues will definitely cause discomfort, especially in companies with a heteropatriarchal status quo. If you publicly call someone out during a meeting, you're going to have to deal with repercussions, whether it's as minor as an eye roll or as major as being taken aside and "spoken to," but I challenge you to do it. I challenge you to think hard about what you're demanding when you stand up for yourself or your colleagues and speak up in meetings or pull someone aside after they've exhibited bullying behavior. If you take the offender aside after the fact, they may brush you off or offer a half-hearted apology because you're not publicly holding them to account in front of other people. If that feels right in the moment and, importantly, safe for you, then do that, but if it happens again, you will have to take further action. You have to demand respect if it's not shown to you or your colleagues, not just because it's right but because it's profoundly empowering. We need to take every opportunity we can to be reminded of our power. Women have been subjugated for far too long, and you have every right to demand your place, to be heard, and to contribute.

Some might say that it shouldn't be the victim's responsibility to take this on, and they're right; we shouldn't have to go through the trauma of publicly shaming every misogynistic, racist bully we come across. It will undoubtedly have a negative impact on our reputations with our colleagues who may feel uncomfortable around us. At some point, they will probably complain that they don't know how to speak to us without causing offense, and ultimately our work environment may sour. Here's what I know to be true: I still carry the memory of all the times I didn't speak up or report incidents, and it doesn't feel good. It feels like shame, anger, and a loss of something integral. I also carry memories of the times I did speak up with me, and those bring me a very different feeling. They give me power, the feeling of carrying light within myself. I don't regret those. I have never once looked back and wished I hadn't spoken up.

I hope that the next time you're in a meeting or having a conversation and someone says something offensive that you won't ignore it, laugh it off, or allow them to feel safe in their behavior. Don't think of their needs and feelings. Remember that your first responsibility is to protect and stand up for yourself and to empower others to speak up for what is right. For years, I went out of my way to make sure that my aggressors felt comfortable in order not to rock the boat, and it has taken a long time for me to finally feel able to say something, to be the person in the room who speaks up for myself and others. When it finally happens, it's a beautiful thing.

Imagine, if you will, a woman on a phone call with her boss: he is clumsily attempting to give her bad news, namely that due to circumstances within the company they work for, her pay will need to be drastically cut for an undefined period of time. As her boss stumbles along, trying to spit out the words the woman already knows are coming, she feels deeply uncomfortable with his unease and decides to step in and make him feel better. She doesn't ask the questions rising within her: "Why is this happening to me and not my male colleagues? You know, the ones who have less experience and no degree? Is this legal?" Instead, she pushes these thoughts down (so they can fester and drown her self-worth in future low moments) while simultaneously pacifying her boss with chirpy platitudes of, "*Of course* the needs of the business come before mine" and "You let me know what you need, and I'll do it!"

Why would she react like this? She's a smart, ambitious woman who works hard to support her family. Why would she happily accept a situation that negatively impacts her and feels deeply unfair? First, because women are trained from childhood to put the needs of others ahead of their own, to nurture, to be nice, to *smile*. When in doubt, our training tells us that it's better for us to be the nice girl than the winner. This is how we are taught to seek approval and love.[140]

Most women have spent a lot of their lives doing the "right thing" in the moment to minimize the discomfort of others, no matter how disastrous the effects of this might be on them personally.[141] That ingrained impulse to always be the good and helpful girl haunts us to the point where some of us may volunteer to fix other people's problems to be perceived as a "helper," even when it's not our responsibility, even when a problem is patently unfixable. Many of us compound this behavior by being unable to receive gratitude or esteem, and we loudly broadcast our inability with obvious discomfort. We signal that we don't need thanking and don't deserve praise. We discount the worth of our efforts and make it clear that we don't feel we deserve honor: "Oh, it's no problem; it was nothing!" If you do any of the above, you probably can't even remember when you started doing it because there's never been a time when you haven't done it. We thank the people who hurt or malign us, tiptoe around the feelings of people who denigrate and demean us. We kiss our executioners because it's more comfortable for us to feel pain than to be perceived as the cause of it in others.

In a series of compelling articles, author Suzannah Weiss describes how many women, in particular Black women and women of Color, are made to feel as though they are not "owed" a life of their own. This feeling multiplies under the constant onslaught of social conditioning that bombards women and rewards "helpfulness" (what society calls female subservience) and emotional disingenuity (always smiling, presenting as "happy" no matter how you actually feel). A "good woman" must always be of service to others and be happy, or at least smile, while she serves others. This negation of self leads to increased levels of anxiety, low self-esteem, and body negativity in women as they continually monitor their actions and appearance in order not to be perceived as a failure.[142]

Continual self-monitoring feeds into society's view that women whose bodies are larger than "normal" are inferior and deficient and stems from a medieval belief that self-control over bodily urges like hunger and sexual desire are indicative of a superior mind and morality. Fast forward seven hundred years, and this idea of control over your desires still exists in today's social conditioning, which uses a person's weight and shape as a marker of their moral code. Society wants men bulky and muscular to take up as much space with their frames as they can while women should be as thin as possible, with those who have literally starved themselves down to the bone held up as a goal. Society tells women that if they just worked a little bit harder, deprived themselves a little bit more, they would become complete and acceptable. The myriad genetic factors behind why many women naturally carry more weight on their frames aren't taken into account; instead, women, young and old alike, are visually bombarded with examples of what a woman should look like. These examples usually show a body type that only 5 percent of women can physically achieve and, even then, is typically found only on the teenage girls or young women in their early twenties who model it. We are assaulted by aspirational images that, for most of us, are physically impossible to achieve, and then we are chastised for not having the moral fiber to attain them. This, combined with the popular media tactic of wielding fatphobic medical research like a club against people deemed to be overweight, leaves many women imbued with a continual sense of shame and distress due to their "moral failure."[143]

The ideal of the "good woman" is also a compelling partner to domestic violence and sexual assault because of how men are taught to view love and sex. In today's society, many of the ways in which cis-het sex is discussed perpetuate objectification, making women a walking target and teaching them that to be attractive is to be a commodity or a trophy to be won by men. As young girls, we're often told that boys are mean to us because they like us—we learn to accept the dichotomy of loving someone who hurts us before we're even remotely old enough to act on those emotions. When we do act on those emotions, we find even more messages of self-negation in which women exist to please men. A 2016 study published in the *Journal of Sex Research* stated that the majority of the seventy-one interviewees (men and women) felt that performing oral sex on women was a "bigger deal" and more "distasteful" than performing oral sex on men and that receiving oral sex was "easier" for men than for women.[144] Women are taught to avoid learning about their own bodies, so they struggle to know what they enjoy while allowing themselves to be used for their partner's pleasure.

Mainstream heteronormative pornography not only amplifies this perception with an emphasis on the importance of male pleasure over female pleasure (i.e., the scene is not "done" until the man climaxes), it also places an emphasis on violent male pleasure. Researcher and author Gail Dines calls pornography "… the perfect propaganda piece for patriarchy" and states that the most popular pornography includes the following acts: vaginal, oral, and anal penetration of a woman by three or more men at the same time; a woman gagging from having a penis thrust down her throat; and ejaculation on a woman's face.[145] Dines believes that pornography drives men toward violence against women, and there looks to be a correlation between men watching a pornographic act and acting it out. In an article by the *Guardian* newspaper, Dines pointed to a collection of studies in 2010 showing that 80 percent of men polled said the sexual act they would most like to act out would be to ejaculate on a woman's face; just three years before, in 2007, on a comment thread of Jezebel.com, a number of women commented that they had experienced their sexual partner ejaculating on their faces without asking permission to do so. There have also been increased numbers of young women reporting anal rape at collegiate sexual assault centers in the US, which Dines attributes to its normalization. She believes "the more porn sexualizes violence against women, the more it normalizes and legitimizes sexually abusive behavior."[146]

For far too long, women have been taught that they're not enough unless they're perpetually happy people-pleasers, sexual objects, and reproductive vessels who give of themselves until they drop from exhaustion. This teaching distracts women from finding their purpose in life, their true calling, whatever that might be. We find ourselves being pulled along in the wake of society's expectations, working in careers that might not feel right for us, with partners who might not really know us, living a life that isn't authentic. Kissing the executioner is merely a symptom of a woman drowning in the unrealistic expectations society places on us, even though we know better than to allow it to happen. Most of us also can't help being sucked into the cult of "likeability" and are deeply invested in whether we are likable, something that most boys and men don't care about. Boys don't care about it because we don't teach them that it's an important part of their character, while girls are raised with it as a central tenet of their character development.[147]

Let's be clear: if you're a woman, especially a Black woman, woman of Color, disabled woman, or a woman from the LGBTQ+ communities, you should be angry. You should be frustrated by women being the most affected by poverty, ill health, abuse, and harassment. You should be angry that women are underrepresented in positions of power and have to play a different game than their male colleagues in the workplace in order to get ahead. An angry woman is someone people find threatening because she cannot be walked over, taken advantage of, or abused. She is powerful in her role of enacting change because she breaks the mold of societal norms. She is deemed to be a bitch, but in the immortal words of Tina Fey: bitches get stuff done.[148]

Here are our favorite ways to stop kissing the executioner and embrace who we are as women.

Staking Your Claim and Just Generally Being Awesome:

1. **Not everyone will like you.** Get over it, babe! The sooner you can absorb this one into your psyche, the better off you'll be. Not every person you work with will like you, and there are a million reasons for this, but 99.99 percent of them will have absolutely nothing to do with who you are as a person. So just get on with your work and cultivate relationships that support you and help you to dynamically evolve into your most authentic self.

2. **Be your authentic self at work.** We know you've probably read a hundred articles telling you to be a social chameleon to get ahead, be whatever and whoever you need to be at that moment. We've tried that approach for decades, and all it does is keep your colleagues from knowing you as a person and bonding with you. Share who you truly are at work, and people who appreciate you will become part of your integral support network and your success partners for the future. We know this can be a scary prospect that, for many women, won't feel safe. All we want to say is that the world deserves the real you, and a workplace that doesn't make you feel safe enough to be your true self isn't safe at all.

3. **Focus on your ability.** Worry less about what your colleagues think of you and focus on honing your specific skill set. Ability, not likeability, should be your ultimate goal. Use the time you would have spent puzzling over why Disco Janet in finance ignores you in the break area and take a training course or read up on something you're curious about. Direct your energy toward things that enhance you as a person because that is where you'll encourage career and personal growth with the most integrity.

4. **Don't be afraid to ask for help.** Sometimes in the corporate world, asking for help can be misinterpreted as weakness or a lack of skill. If you're feeling overwhelmed or have a knowledge gap, reaching out to a colleague will not only create a bond between the two of you, but also boost you both emotionally. You, because you're being supported, and your colleague, because they're able to offer support and feel needed. Double whammy. Important to note that not all colleagues are suitable for this. You'll need to find someone that you like and respect. If that's not possible in your current workplace, then first, think about quitting (seriously), and second, have a look on LinkedIn or search for local meet-ups for people in your field. If you're stuck in a rut, you may need to search a bit further afield to find the right hand to help you up. As they say in France, "C'est vaut le voyage." It's worth the trip.

To learn more, please check out these additional resources:

Books

- Carruthers, Charlene. *Unapologetic: A Black, Queer, and Feminist Mandate for Radical Movements.* Boston: Beacon Press, 2019.
- Conger, Cristen, and Carolina Ervin. *Unladylike: A Field Guide to Smashing the Patriarchy and Claiming Your Space.* California: Ten Speed Press, 2018.
- Jones, Feminista. *Reclaiming Our Space: How Black Feminists Are Changing the World from the Tweets to the Streets.* Boston: Beacon Press, 2019.

Activists/ Influencers

- Feminist Bro
  - Instagram @thisisfeministbro
- Feminista Jones
  - Instagram @feministajones
  - www.feministajones.com
- Insterscetional Feminist *she/her*
  - Instagram @feministwarrior_

CHAPTER 10
CONTROLLED BY FEAR

It's men who trust they will suffer no consequences for their actions, while women suffer no matter what they do.
–MEGHAN MACLEAN WEIR

t's different for everyone. When you're on an airplane flying through particularly heavy turbulence and the plane "falls" a few feet. When your car hydroplanes on the highway during a heavy storm. When a massive spider drops down an inch from your face. Many women feel it when they walk across a darkened parking lot or down a poorly lit street on their own. Sometimes it rises up when we walk past or through a cluster of men. Fear is the most effective tool you can use to control or modify a person's behavior, and it has been used for millennia to dominate and silence women. As we discussed in chapter 3, the control of women is a key tenet of a patriarchal social construct, so understanding how women are controlled by fear is hugely important. The most consistent experiences of fear and control that women have over their lifetimes are those of sexual harassment and violence. We recognize these topics might be triggering for many readers; please know that it was incredibly difficult for us to write this chapter, not just because of our personal experiences but because of our driving need to do justice to the experiences of our sisters, friends, daughters, mothers, aunts, cousins, and grandmothers. We need to be talking about this because it happens to women around the world on a daily basis, in the home and in the workplace, and it affects the trajectory of our personal and professional lives. This is a hugely emotive subject for many women, including us, so we thought it would be easier to delve into it by starting with facts instead of a personal story.

Let's start outside: in a survey of 811 women by the NPO Stop Street Harassment (SSH), 90 percent had experienced street harassment by the age of nineteen.[149]

Another SSH survey of 2,000 women found that 81 percent had been sexually harassed in their lifetimes:[150]

- **76 percent** said that the sexual harassment was verbal.
- **49 percent** were sexually touched without their permission.
- **40 percent** were sexually harassed online.
- **30 percent** faced unwanted genital flashing.
- **27 percent** were physically followed.

These women were affected by their experiences of sexual harassment in the following ways:[151]

- **30 percent** reported feeling anxious or depressed.
- **23 percent** changed their regular routines or routes.
- **22 percent** ended a relationship, either with a friend or partner.
- **10 percent** filed an official report with an authority figure such as the police.
- **9 percent** either changed or quit their jobs or looked for a new job assignment.
- **7 percent** sought medical help, including counseling.
- **5 percent** stopped participating in their community or engaging in hobbies or activities.
- **5 percent** moved out of their house, dorm, or apartment.

- **2 percent** changed or dropped out of school or a specific course.
- **1 percent** confronted the offender.

Surveyed women said they first experienced sexual harassment at the following ages:[152]
- **18 percent** ten years old and younger
- **51 percent** eleven to thirteen years old
- **24 percent** fourteen to sixteen years old
- **7 percent** older than sixteen years old

When you look at those figures, it's hard to imagine why more women don't speak out about these experiences (though Tarana Burke's "Me Too," Soma Sara's "Everyone's Invited," and the "Time's Up" movements are helping to shift the needle) and why we aren't holding men accountable for this kind of behavior. Yes, men get sexually harassed as well, but women are disproportionately affected by it, which is what we're discussing here.

One of the most consistent issues that we have come across in our research on sexual harassment is that men and women have very different ideas about what constitutes sexual harassment. For men in general, unless the sexual harassment is extreme, like sexual coercion through impairing substances like drugs and alcohol, or putting undue pressure on a woman to acquiesce, they don't view it as sexual harassment. When a man watches another man repeatedly pressure a woman for a date, make an unwanted sexual comment to her, or touch her without permission, he will tend not to regard it as sexual harassment, though a woman would. Men are also more likely to think that a woman is lying about, or exaggerating the experience of, sexual harassment, or that they are to blame for sexual harassment because of their behavior (provocative manner, not clearly discouraging a man's advances, etc.) or the way they dress.[153] We don't think we have to remind any women reading this of what can happen if you do clearly discourage a man's sexual advances! It will also come as no surprise that many women who are sexually harassed often get gaslit by their attackers if they react in their own defense. Typically, these women (we're speaking from experience here) are told that it was just a bit of fun, a joke, nothing to get so upset about. They're asked why they don't have a sense of humor. Why make such a big deal out of nothing?

For the avoidance of doubt, let's define what sexual harassment is: unwanted conduct of a sexual nature which has the purpose or effect of violating someone's dignity or creating an intimidating, hostile, degrading, humiliating, or offensive environment for them. This includes, but is not limited to, the following acts:[154]

- Indecent or suggestive remarks, questions, jokes, or suggestions about a colleague's sex life
- The display of pornography in the workplace
- The circulation of pornography
- Unwelcome and inappropriate touching, hugging, or kissing
- Requests or demands for sexual favors
- Treating someone less favorably because they have rejected or submitted to unwanted sexual conduct
- Any unwelcome behavior of a sexual nature that creates an intimidating, hostile, or humiliating working environment

According to a Pew Research Center survey on sexual harassment in the workplace, women working in male-dominated workplaces are more likely to experience sexual harassment (surprise!).[155] When sexual harassment occurs in the workplace, its negative impact is amplified because of the closed environment it occurs in. For Black women and women of Color, sexual harassment is even more powerful because it can be both a sexual attack and a racist one, while LGBTQ+ women can simultaneously experience sexual harassment and homophobic, biphobic, or transphobic harassment.

Disabled women between the ages of eighteen and thirty-four have an incredibly high rate of workplace harassment, with 78 percent reporting being sexually harassed.[156] The Trade Union Congress (TUC) reported in 2020 that:[157]

- One in two women experienced sexual harassment in the workplace.
- Two in three LGBTQ+ workers experienced sexual harassment in the workplace.
- Four out of five people don't feel able to report sexual harassment to their employer.

The TUC's previous report in 2016 disclosed the following:[158]

- More than half (52 percent) of all women polled have experienced some form of sexual harassment.
- 35 percent of women have heard comments of a sexual nature being made about other women in the workplace.
- 32 percent of women have been subject to unwelcome jokes of a sexual nature.
- 28 percent of women have been subject to comments of a sexual nature about their body or clothes.
- Nearly 25 percent of women have experienced unwanted touching (such as a hand on the knee or lower back).
- 20 percent of women have experienced unwanted sexual advances.
- More than one in ten women reported experiencing unwanted sexual touching or attempts to kiss them.
- Nearly one in five women reported that their direct manager or someone else with direct authority over them was the perpetrator.
- Four out of five women did not report the sexual harassment to their employer.

Four out of five women works out to roughly 80 percent. Why would nearly all of the women who experienced sexual harassment not report it? One major reason is that, for a woman, reporting sexual harassment can be a double-edged sword: You may want to report it, but the consequences of reporting harassment can be seriously detrimental to a woman's career, especially when her attacker is in a senior position to her. This is especially true in male-dominated industries or workplaces, where men tend to occupy senior roles or positions of power and women tend to be in junior or support roles. Nearly 75 percent of women who reported their sexual harassment said that there were no visible repercussions for the perpetrator, and 16 percent of the women who reported their sexual harassment said that they were treated worse as a result of reporting.[159] An estimated 66 percent of disabled women sexually harassed at work didn't report it, with the most common reason being that they didn't think they would be believed.[160]

In the TUC 2016 study, women stated the following reasons for not reporting sexual harassment:[161]

- 30 percent of women said that they feared that reporting the incident would have a negative impact on their working relationships.
- Nearly 25 percent said that they did not think they would be believed or taken seriously.
- 20 percent said they were too embarrassed to report it.
- 15 percent feared a negative impact on their career if they reported it.
- 12 percent said they did not know how to report the unwanted behavior.
- 10 percent said they were unaware that they could report it.

As startling as it is to think that so many women didn't realize they could report sexual harassment or didn't know how to, the TUC study also found that 37 percent of women polled said they didn't report their sexual harassment for a reason that wasn't listed.[162] The list included negative impact on career, work relationships, not being taken seriously or being blamed, embarrassment, not knowing that you could report or how to do so, and preferring not to say. That's a very comprehensive list; however, there was one reason missing from their list that we hear pretty consistently, said in a multitude of ways: it's just the way things are, it's always been this way, it's Boys' Club, etc.

There is a widespread belief that this is how men behave, especially among older women who worked in the corporate world decades before sexual harassment was taken seriously an offensive act. Often, the mindset we've found that older women have about sexual harassment in the workplace is that it's something women just need to accept and move on from if they want to "play with the big boys." While we appreciate and sympathize with these women, many of whom were probably put through hell during their working careers, this isn't the right way to look at the situation. This kind of behavior is unacceptable anywhere but especially in the workplace, where it negatively impacts the careers and financial stability of the victims disproportionately more than the aggressors. We cannot be complacent or accepting of it, and yes, we know we discussed complacency in chapter 7, and we appreciate how hard it is to overcome. Still, when it comes to your safety at work, complacency can truly harm you.

Here's Jenni's experience of sexual harassment. We hope you're ready to hear it.

Jenni's Story:

Women of all ages have experienced some form of sexual harassment in the workplace. It can range from "innocent" jokes, to threats, to full-on unwanted touch. I have experienced the entire spectrum and, for many years, took it in my stride, not wanting to call attention to it for fear of embarrassing my abuser and potentially losing my job.

Whatever your experience is with sexual harassment, assault, or abuse, I want to make a few things clear:

- *It's not your fault.*
- *Whatever you feel is valid.*
- *Do not internalize this—tell HR, talk to your coworkers, confide in your support system.*

Our attackers wield all the power in these situations because that's how the paradigm is set up: sexual harassment is used more often as a power play than for sexual gratification. Women who have been harassed or assaulted in the workplace are left feeling completely violated and fearful. Whatever emotions you feel about your experience are the right ones, and it's of the utmost importance to share with someone you trust, once you're ready.

What you don't get told, but should know, is that once you report your harassment or assault, you may feel incredibly alienated as the mechanism of patriarchal control rears its ugly head. It may come from people you would never have believed to be so deeply entrenched in something that so obviously works against them. Those who have the courage to report assault or harassment are usually viewed by outsiders as bearing some kind of responsibility for the incident having happened. It's victim-blaming, pure and simple, and it consistently happens in situations like these.

When I reported a man who was constantly inappropriate, not just with me but many of my female and male colleagues, I immediately became the office outcast. My one saving grace, if it can be called that, was that I had suffered a stillbirth around the same time, which humanized me and made me harder to hate. The truth is that no one who knew about my report was surprised that I had done it because this guy was a complete pervert who got away with terrible behavior because of his senior position in the company. Eventually, he was let go during a period of major restructuring, and I remember the COO making eye contact with me when he had gathered the team together to tell them the news of his departure. Keeping his eye on me, he told us that no one was let go because they'd done anything wrong, and I was immediately seething but stayed silent, feeling ashamed and doubting whether I had been right to report him.

My advice to anyone going through this is to seek out a support system and find a way to vent your emotions in a way that will empower you. Write, cry, scream, do anything you need to in order to make it through the low moments. Speak to a therapist and keep your loved ones close to help move you through it. I didn't sue the company I worked for, but when I eventually quit to get away from the toxic environment, I was able to get unemployment benefits. The company tried to fight back, but luckily, my case was reviewed by an amazing, compassionate man who listened to my story, believed me, and approved my claim.

Here's what I did right:

- *I documented everything I was going through—when I finally spoke to my HR department, I brought a long list of dates and details of when my harasser had been inappropriate with me. I could have been a bit more comprehensive in recording the fall out I experienced after I reported him, but in general, I managed to capture the majority of the harassment.*

- *I contacted friends in the legal profession—they gave me good advice, but more importantly, these conversations validated my experiences and helped solidify the feeling that I was not in the wrong. It is so important to hang on to this feeling, especially if there's a backlash against you after reporting.*

- *I kept showing up to work—I kept my head held high even on the days when this was hard to do as my harasser was behaving passive-aggressively and I had no support from either HR or my managers. I did my job as best I could and let the shit-talking happen behind my back while constantly reminding myself that I was in the right. I vented to friends and family whenever I needed to in order to keep myself centered.*

- *I went to counseling—Therapy was a lifesaver through all of this. Having an outlet to release your emotions is essential, especially when you're in the eye of the storm and every day feels like a battle for survival. Finding a professional resource to rely on as you go through this is so worth it; you will need it.*

Here are some things I could have done better:
- *I should have documented everything that happened from the very beginning, before it got explicit. Every inappropriate conversation, every experience where I walked away uncomfortable, along with the date, the time, the location, and anyone who might have seen or heard it happening.*
- *I should have trusted myself and reported right away.*
- *I should have confronted him sooner.*
- *I should have reported them all: the manager who told me, via Messenger, that he wanted me "so fucking bad" at 9:00 a.m. when I worked as his assistant, and I closed the chat window thinking he'd made a mistake; or the boss who would stand next to my desk and tell other men how he punished his wife with anal sex then make comments about my shoes and clothes. I should have reported the man who, during an interview that I had to beg to get, asked why I was getting married when I could have any man I wanted. When I made it clear I was only interested in the job (not him), he told me that I was unqualified for the role even though I had years of experience; he had never even bothered to look at my resume.*

At the time these situations were happening, I told myself it wouldn't have mattered if I reported them. I worked for companies with poor HR teams in environments controlled by men, and if I had reported the men who harassed or assaulted me, they would only have branded me a troublemaker and pushed me out the door.

Knowing all of this, I can tell you one thing: reporting what happened was right, and I have (finally) stopped blaming myself. I stood up and made a lot of people uncomfortable because I was brave enough to call out unacceptable behavior in the workplace. I did the right thing, not just for myself but for others in the company who were affected by this man's disgusting behavior, and I'm proud of myself. Reporting was scary and very isolating but was 100 percent worth it. I'd do it again in a heartbeat, but hopefully, I won't have to.

We discussed in chapter 3 that within a patriarchal society, women and their sexuality must be controlled, so it should come as no surprise that sexual harassment is all about power. It can be used by the attacker to increase their own feelings of power and status as well as a tool to disenfranchise others. Women who were sexually harassed in the workplace reported feeling shame, guilt, and a sense of being undermined professionally; these feelings were heightened when the sexual harassment took place in front of other colleagues. The fact that women on temporary contracts, working through agencies, or on zero-hours contracts are more likely to experience certain types of harassment and less likely to report it further underlines that sexual harassment is about power as you cannot find a woman with less power than one in a precarious work situation.

So how do we get over this one? It's a pretty colossal hurdle involving transformative change at the personal level as well as within company cultures and society at large.

Scumbag Eradication System (and Social Awareness Upgrade):

1. **All hands on deck.** There needs to be a cohesive company-wide approach, which means one supported by everyone from the directors and board members to the employees, to sexual harassment in the workplace. There should be a clear sexual harassment policy that explains what sexual harassment is and details the process for filing a complaint, including who to report to, what the person filing the complaint can expect to see happen, and what timescale to expect. This information should be made freely available to all employees and should be provided to all new employees within their induction pack. If this does not exist in your company, you need to demand it. If it does exist, ask that a "refresh" is done for the whole company in order to bring it to the forefront. Don't be surprised if people are annoyed at you for asking for this. Some companies have domineering or oppressive toxic work cultures that do not like having to put on this kind of public "show." If you remain strong and publicly demand accountability, action will have to be taken.

2. **Train the team.** Everyone needs to be trained on what sexual harassment is, including stalking and online harassment, and how to report it, but those entrusted with protecting employees, like those working in HR or any managerial role, need to have further in-depth training. This includes learning about the relevant state or federal laws governing sexual harassment, reviewing the company's policies, and being trained on how to handle the entire complaint process.

3. **Everyone is accountable.** There needs to be zero tolerance for sexual harassment built into the company culture,

which means that people who are reported for harassment are met with serious consequences that are visible to the entire company. This is not an unnecessary shaming. It is sending a clear message to all employees that their safety is paramount to the company, and it is a serious matter. This is especially important if further grievances occur after an incident is reported, such as harassment increasing after being reported or if the victim is treated negatively by any team members after reporting. Employees should know and see that the company is dedicated to maintaining a safe space for them, even if that means disciplining or firing a board member or director.

5. **Show that all employees are equal.** Anyone with job insecurity is vulnerable and easier to abuse: protect all employees with permanent contracts for good pay and sensible, flexible working hours. Agency workers or people on temporary or zero-hour contracts are not in secure employment. These should only be used for emergency situations on a short-term basis. A dedicated workforce is one that is invested in their company because their company protects and nurtures them.

If You Only Remember Two Things, Make It These Two:

1. **Report *everything*.** It doesn't matter if it's the company owner, and you think he was probably joking: *report him*. If it made you or a colleague feel intimidated, humiliated, demeaned, embarrassed, or offended, then it's not appropriate behavior, and it needs to be reported. If you see someone touch someone inappropriately, report them. Let the HR team sort out precisely what happened and what the real story is. Not everyone will feel capable of reporting sexual harassment. This is especially true of people who

have experienced sexual abuse or childhood trauma, which carry narratives of guilt, shame, and unworthiness that may prevent them from advocating for themselves. If you can find a safe way to do so, we urge you to use your voice even though it will feel very uncomfortable. Complacency in this kind of situation impacts not just the victims who are unable to speak out but also the young people who will join the company and might be taught that these behaviors are acceptable.

2. **Know when to call it a day.** You may well be the only voice in a company asking for this to be considered an important issue at first, but if, after a period of time, you realize that the company does not value this kind of employee protection, then it's probably not a safe place to work. Companies show their true colors when they decide how to spend their HR and training budgets: either they're actively working to make your work life a safe, positive experience, or they don't deserve your mind and your skill set.

To learn more, please check out these additional resources:

Books

- Carlson, Gretchen. *Be Fierce: Stop Harassment and Take Your Power Back*. New York: Center Street, 2017.

Activists/ Influencers

- End Violence Against Women UK
  - Instagram @evawuk
  - www.endviolenceagainstwomen.org.uk

- Every 2 Minutes
  - Instagram @every2min
- Me Too Many Voices Community Support Network
  - Instagram @mtmvcommunity
  - www.mtmvsupport.org
- Our Streets Now
  - Instagram @ourstreetsnow
  - TikTok @ourstreetsnow1
  - www.ourstreetsnow.com
- Safe Bae
  - Instagram @safe_bae
  - www.safebae.org
- The Catcall Collective *she/her*
  - Instagram @thecatcallcollective

CHAPTER 11
WHO CARES FOR THE CARETAKERS?

Caring for myself is not self-indulgence,
it is self-preservation, and that is an act of political warfare.
—AUDRE LORD

Jenni's Story:

The other day, I asked my husband how much his life had changed since we had children. Not in meaningless little ways, like how much sleep are you getting, how many diapers are you changing, how much laundry are you doing? I was curious about how he noticed his life had changed since he became a parent because he still gets up in the morning, goes to work, and clocks in his nine-to-five. Did he feel different about himself, I wondered? Were there different expectations of him after becoming a father? He shrugged and said it really hadn't changed much and that he doesn't feel the weight of any additional expectations either. I can't imagine ever getting that response from a mother: our entire lives change, and not just because of the complete lack of sleep and privacy, but because of the massive mental and emotional load we place on women who choose to become mothers. It's a deluge of judgment, criticism, and societal expectations of being the perfect, *crunchy mom. Perfectly coiffed and manicured with a new baby hanging off your perky tits that have snapped back immediately along with your stomach, hips, and all other (rapidly shrinking) body parts.*

Unlike my husband, my life has become unrecognizable in the seven years since I became a mother. It transformed the moment I had my first baby, pre-childbirth me became a distant memory, and I know too many women who are in the same boat. Women from older generations like to say that fathers today are so much more involved, but honestly, nothing has really changed in the last thirty years. I have a very helpful partner, but his life remained pretty uncomplicated until the time when he, by choice, took a brief reprieve from paid work to take on extra parental duties. When we switched places, I, the breadwinner, returned to work, and he stayed home. The backlash was swift and severe. Judgment was heaped on me for emasculating him (WTF), some of his friends expressed disappointment in him, and his family worried about the career impact of his decision. Where was the outrage for my career penalty or the concern for my once-promising future?

For new fathers, the status quo quickly returns, but for new mothers, it's a whole new world. As we've discussed in previous chapters, it's typically mothers who leave work when the kids get sick, work from home on the days that the kids are off school, or take those days off completely. Even on vacation, my husband works and then joins us when he's done, but I am stuck in a constant loop of parenthood twenty-four hours a day, seven days a week.

Who cares for the caretakers? For many women, being an unpaid caretaker is a harsh reality, and their needs never get met, much less acknowledged. This is why the mantra of self-care has been reduced to eating regularly, drinking water, washing ourselves, and other basic human needs because some days moms don't even have time for those. The sad thing is that, for the most part, there's no one out there, other than other caretakers, even thinking about our needs or that this perpetual unpaid work, which enables the world's economies to exist and function, is killing us.

We know that the societal expectation of women is that they are of service at all times: a vessel to create children and a lifelong servant to their needs, the perfect host and homemaker, sexual objects for our partners, and yet also, somehow, completely committed to our careers. It is impossible for one person to fulfill all of these roles. When we get caught up in trying, we lose ourselves in the process because this hopeless ambition to be everything to all people demands that we deny ourselves the care and comfort we need and deserve. Many of us have not been taught the importance of self-care for our mental, emotional, and physical health, much less shown how to actively and regularly engage in it. A core objective of self-care is getting your head, heart, and body in tune with each other, something which is being destroyed by leading the hyper-busy, stressful lives that many of us find ourselves in. We need to look at ourselves holistically: what negatively impacts us physically also affects our emotional and mental processes. So let's start from the top and work our way down.

Did you know that women are twice as likely as men to have anxiety? We also make up 60 percent of people who suffer from phobias or obsessive-compulsive disorder, both of which are classed as anxiety disorders. On average, women are more likely to suffer from income, housing, and health-care inequalities, and because of this, we are disproportionately affected by mental health disorders. One in four women will seek treatment for depression over their lifetimes, and because of our excessive exposure to sexual abuse and violence, women are twice as likely to be affected by PTSD as men. Immoderate stress levels can encourage or exacerbate existing, poor mental health. For women, if they are struggling to create a work-life balance or have an unsympathetic workplace, the impact is devastating.[163]

Even before the hammer blow of the COVID-19 pandemic, women's mental health in the corporate environment wasn't in a good place. In January 2020, a report released by *Woman's Day* showed staggering figures: 80 percent of the women surveyed said that either they or a loved one had dealt with mental health challenges; 54 percent said that they didn't discuss mental health issues at work for fear of career penalty; and 73 percent said they knew it needed to be talked about (but wasn't).[164] In March 2021, the HOW Institute issued a "Human Connection" report which stated that while overall only 44 percent of workers reported feeling less connected to coworkers than they did in March 2020, 100 percent of the women surveyed reported feeling disconnected from colleagues, line managers, or the companies they worked for. The report cited researchers Nicole Bateman and Martha Ross in their Brookings Institution report, which stated that because women were already disproportionately bearing the burden of domestic and care work before the pandemic struck, the closure of childcare settings increased that burden, making it more difficult for mothers working outside the home to engage and connect at work.[165]

While working mothers were already twice as likely as working fathers to worry about garnering career penalties because of their caregiving responsibilities, working women in senior roles are now burning out at a rate of 39 percent compared to 28 percent of men. When we add in the ramifications of non-inclusive working environments, Black women suffer the most, not least because 50 percent say they are the only Black woman in their particular role at the company they work for. In addition to the continual onslaught of violence against Black people and people of Color, and constant media coverage of it, along with the daily impact of systemic racism, it should come as no surprise that Black women are the most likely to feel uncomfortable speaking to their colleagues about stress or grief and the least likely to feel safe enough to show themselves truly at work.[166] Black women are also more likely to feel like they have no allies in the workplace, so it should come as no surprise that Black women experience depression twice as often as Black men. Women of Color are also disproportionately negatively impacted by depression and poor mental health but are less likely to be perceived as requiring mental health services. When systemic racism and misogyny intersect, it leaves Black women and women of Color more likely to have low-income jobs and multiple job strain, both of which increase the risk of poor mental health.[167]

From a physiological perspective, when we run ourselves into the ground through lack of sleep and excessive stress, we weaken our immune systems and encourage inflammation to grow in our bodies. This leads to an increased risk of developing autoimmune diseases, depression, diabetes, and heart disease, as well as sleep and digestive disorders. Recent research has flagged that women's preventive health care was knocked off course by the pandemic with routine cervical and breast cancer screenings postponed across the globe, leading researchers and practitioners to raise the alarm that cancer rates could jump in years to come.[168]

In the UK specifically, the *Lancet Oncology* journal projected that due to diagnostic delays in 2020, breast cancer deaths could jump as much as 9.6 percent in the next five years.[169] So now, women are expected to dedicate themselves to their jobs, families, children (if they have them), and households, *and* be "proactively vigilant about their own mental and physical healthcare."[170] If it sounds and feels like too much, it's because it is. We have to ask: Who is caring for *us*? Who cares for the caretakers? How can we nourish ourselves when our own cup is empty from nourishing others?

For the record, washing your hair, drinking water, eating regular meals, and sleeping more than four hours a night is not self-care. That is meeting our basic human needs, and it will not revive your spirit or refill your cup. Achieving that level of rejuvenation can only happen when you truly care for yourself by engaging your inner creative (and yes, we all have one), taking yourself away for silence or isolation when you're feeling touched out, speaking to a mental health practitioner, etc. For many of us, these experiences are encouraged by our friends, family, and society, but only as a one-off. Unfortunately, one-time activities will not result in our cups magically filling back up and staying filled; in fact, doing one-time activities may make you feel even worse afterward because of the crushing guilt that comes because you haven't been healed, transformed, replenished by a solitary act. A one-off is never going to be enough for a full system reset. True self-care is habitual. Be patient with yourself. Take the time and space you need to make balance and joy part of your life again, in whatever way works for you.

No one can dictate what you should be feeling, how much energy you should have, or that you should be thankful for getting five minutes alone in the shower. You're allowed to be tired and fed up. If you have daily care duties, you're allowed to feel sad and mourn the woman you were before you became a full-time caretaker. Taking the time to pause, reflect on how you're feeling, and look for ways to replenish yourself and find joy in your life is essential. Without this regular self-check-in, you'll be perpetually running on empty. Surround yourself with things that give back to you, whether that's friends, family, or activities. Clean up your life by removing the people and things that drain you or fill you with anxiety or doubt. It's okay to say goodbye to what doesn't serve you. Many of us have been running on empty for so long that it might take months, even years, of concerted effort to find our way back to ourselves, to accept and nurture the woman we have evolved into. Don't let anyone dictate who that woman is or make you feel guilty for taking care of yourself. Society and the media are always ready to tear women down—eliminate any part of your daily life that makes you feel shitty or less than. To quote the beautifully succinct Sweet Brown: "Ain't nobody got time for that."[171]

One of the ways women tend to de-stress or get through hard times is by talking it out. Being "over-communicators" is one of the most consistent stereotypes about women, and while this can be used as a disparaging comment in professional situations (i.e., "Chatty Cathy," "mother's meeting," etc.), the very real tendency of women to naturally support each other through social networks and communicate our issues is actually an asset in the corporate environment. It makes us good listeners, empathetic leaders, and sets us up to create more welcoming workplaces than have existed in the past. Empathy, in particular, is lauded as one of the core "soft skills" good leaders should have but is often still maligned as weakness when displayed in heteropatriarchal corporate settings. This phenomenon ties in strongly with the way boys are not encouraged to nurture others and express themselves emotionally in the way that girls are. Such an approach helps create men who are unreceptive to others' feelings or ideas, are hypercritical, socially awkward, and tend to make uninformed decisions. Hands up if you've ever worked with a man like that—we certainly have come across a few in our time. Women's typical communication style, both innate and learned, is such a defining characteristic that when we are in stressful or threatening situations, we are more apt to engage with those around us, specifically other women and children, to better support them. Known as "tend and befriend," it's a relatively new understanding of women's natural stress response and is in direct opposition to the accepted stress response of "fight or flight," which was based on a single research study conducted in 1932 looking at the responses of male rats. Since then, further studies have been conducted but have used men's responses as the majority, with women only representing 17 percent of the participants. As a historical aside, the reason the majority of past research studies have focused on cisgender men's responses has been that menstruating people have a much more complex and varied response to environmental stress due to their cyclical variations—

so data drawn from people who menstruate can present confusing or inconsistent results.[172] In short, we're hard work.

Chances are that if you were assigned female at birth, you were taught from a very young age to be quiet, nice, and humble. Society doesn't usually approve of loud girls, bossy girls, arrogant girls, or girls who are too smart "for their own good." In general, girls are encouraged to play with dolls and baby carriages, while boys play with trucks and soldiers. Girls are given dollhouses, and boys get toolboxes.[173] These were the ingredients we were given as young girls in order to form us into the "right" kind of woman.

It was at the young age of three or four that we first met and played with our most impactful toys: dolls, particularly those whose body proportions were completely unrealistic. Our doll of choice from childhood was Barbie, who, if her body ratios were scaled up to human proportions, would have a sixteen-inch waist (bye-bye internal organs!) and thigh circumference, a nine-inch neck unable to support her head, six-inch ankles unable to support her weight, and three-and-a-half-inch wrists incapable of lifting anything. This mutated version of a woman was held up to us as the ultimate form of a glamorous and beautiful woman. How could we not internalize this first ruinous lesson that being skinny made us desirable and more deserving of love?

When we grew out of playing with Barbies, our attention was turned to the live-action variety: we consumed teen magazines packed with images of real models showing us what a woman should look like. Fashion models averaging out at 5'9" with a twenty-three-inch waist and weighing 23 percent less than the average American woman with a BMI of seventeen, which is medically defined as being "underweight" and associated with thinning bones, lack of period, infertility, heart arrhythmia, and increased risk of heart attack.[174] Fifty-five percent of fashion models start between the ages of thirteen to sixteen[175] yet are used to represent what an adult woman should look like, though *Vogue* magazine recently pledged to stop using models under eighteen.[176] Over 50 percent of American women are a size 14 or larger, yet fashion models wear an American size 0 or 2, and the majority of women's clothing stores do not stock or sell clothing in sizes larger than 12 or 14.[177] While we applaud the growth of body neutrality and positivity movements, along with the surge in popularity of mainstream artists like Lizzo, there is still a global lack of recognition and acceptance of what the "average woman" looks like. For example, the "Curvy Barbie" released in 2016, meant to herald the inclusion of diverse body shapes, is still three sizes smaller than the average British woman.[178] There will be readers who will want to point us toward the rise of body positivity and body neutrality on social media, and yes, you can find body-positive and body-neutral accounts and influencers to follow if you look for them. Overwhelmingly though, the research points to social media negatively impacting the body image of teenage girls in particular who, when they feel bad about their bodies, feel even worse when they use Instagram.[179] Compound this with being unable to find clothes above a certain size (14 in both the US and the UK) in many stores or shopping malls in spite of the fact that the average American woman wears a size 16 or 18,[180] and the average British woman wears a size 16.[181] At this point, most women and girls succumb to societal pressures and usher in the profoundly flawed influence of modern weight-loss culture.

Weight loss culture, at its core, influences women to actively work to make themselves smaller in order to fit what society says a woman should be, not what they truly are. Please know that you are doing the work of the Patriarchy when you push your body toward its skinniest possible version—hips and collar bones protruding, starving yourself down to nothing in order to achieve the elusive thigh gap. As an aside, having a thigh gap is entirely dependent on the width of your hips compared to the length of your femoral head (the ball at the top of your femur), so for many women it's not even possible to have a thigh gap unless they completely decimate the muscle mass of their thighs through extreme starvation.

Believe us when we say that we bought into this patriarchal lie and deeply internalized the need to be skin and bones in order to become the ultimate version of ourselves as "valuable" women. We took diet pills by the handful from the age of twelve, our hands shaking from the continuous jolt of ephedrine coursing through our veins. When those were banned by the FDA in the early 2000s, we moved on to diuretics, cleanses, and fasts endorsed by celebrities, bought chitin pills and ate cabbage soup for breakfast, lunch, and dinner for weeks at a time. If we had to eat a fattening meal with family or friends, we would sneak off to the bathroom to throw up, and when it was easier to get away with than we thought it would be, it became a regular part of our daily routine for years. We smoked cigarettes instead of eating, we chewed ice instead of eating, we took drugs instead of eating, and guess what? We lost weight, as you do when you starve yourself, and felt amazing when our shrunken stomachs made it easier for us to refuse normal amounts of food. We loved the feeling of being skinny and whole-heartedly bought into Kate Moss's anthem for our generation: "Nothing tastes as good as skinny feels."[182] Sadly, nothing ever seemed to keep the weight off permanently; it was almost like our bodies didn't want to be reduced to skin and bones. We had to keep searching for more extreme ways of removing the extra weight from our frames that began to build up more quickly as we aged—annoyingly, our bodies seemed to be working overtime to keep us from starving them to death. Weight-loss culture preys on this terrible obsession and continually spawns new forms of self-annihilation, like the creation and surreptitious promotion of pro-ana (pro-anorexic) and pro-mia (pro-bulimia), both grievous and heart-breaking symptoms of the oppression under which many young girls, and some young men, starve and die.

Know this: the Patriarchy wants you small and quiet, meek and humble. Too hungry to be aware of the world around you. Too insecure to speak up for your rights and the rights of your sisters. In her seminal work, *The Beauty Myth*, Naomi Wolf wrote that powerful, aware women are a threat to our social construct. Neither capitalism nor the patriarchy benefit from women who reject the impossible beauty standards of today's society. Wolf went on to say that as long as women are consumed by the oppression and diminishment of their own bodies, they will never truly be free.[183]

It will come as no surprise to some of our readers that within today's workplace, there is no protection for people with bodies deemed to be larger than "normal." It's legal in forty-eight US states to discriminate against someone in the workplace because of their weight, and there is no federal law against weight-based discrimination.[184] There is no legal protection from weight-based workplace discrimination in UK or EU law. A study done at Harvard showed that, as opposed to race, gender, and sexual orientation, participants recorded increased discrimination against those of larger body types over the course of a decade.[185] Anti-fatness is well entrenched in our society, accepted in the workplace, and, unsurprisingly, on the rise.

We need to say that the word "fat," which has held a negative connotation in Western societies for the last few decades, wasn't always viewed as such. Even going back just a century or so, we find that beauty standards included being fat as a key part of visual appeal and a sign of wealth.[186] Now, however, we use the word "fat" as an insult instead of a neutral descriptor, and women in particular shy away from using the word because of the negative subtext it carries and the way we all see fat people in society being treated. Fat people are made the butt of jokes. They are the victims of weight-based "concern trolling" where people (usually strangers) attempt to undermine their autonomy and their intelligence by questioning their general health and the dietary choices they make. With relief in our voices, we assure ourselves and our friends that we're "not fat" as if being fat was the worst thing you could be. As if being fat wasn't the lived experience of millions of people who recognize themselves in a word which so many people use as an insult. In the words of Aubrey Gordon (@YrFatFriend on Instagram), "When you cannot name our bodies, when you cannot regard our skin neutrally, what chance do you have of treating us respectfully or lovingly?"[187]

Knowing all of this, is it any wonder that weight-based discrimination in the workplace is able to fly under the radar? One of the main reasons why is that many people believe that being fat is a choice. The majority of employers are still very likely to think that it's caused by poor lifestyle choices and that it is preventable. Research done on weight-based discrimination found that study participants rated fat job applicants as lacking self-discipline, having low supervisory potential, poor personal hygiene, and poor professional appearance.[188] A 2012 poll conducted on 2,300 American adults by Harris Interactive and Health Day found that 52 percent of the fat people polled felt they had experienced weight-based discrimination when applying for a job or promotion. Sixty-one percent of the total respondents of the poll felt that making negative remarks about another person's weight wasn't offensive.[189]

Studies of fat women living in the UK found that 25 percent had reported experiencing weight-based discrimination in the workplace, 54 percent reported weight-based stigma from their colleagues, and 43 percent reported weight-based discrimination from their employers. Sixty percent of fat women who had reported weight-based discrimination had experienced this kind of discrimination four times or more during their working careers.[190]

Research done at Vanderbilt University found that fat women earn less than their thin colleagues, on average. This study found that fat women were more likely to have jobs that emphasized physical activity and less likely to have jobs that emphasized public interaction. Because jobs that emphasize physical activity tend to pay less than jobs that emphasize public interaction, there is a wage penalty for fat women, not to mention that when fat women do work in "front-facing" roles, they are paid less than their thin colleagues. It's important to note that these career patterns are not the same for fat men.[191]

When you're constantly deluged by discrimination, it takes a considerable toll on your health. A study conducted on nearly 20,000 participants in their midlife and retirement age showed a 60 percent increase in mortality risk to people living with weight-based discrimination, which was not accounted for by common physical or psychological factors. Put bluntly, living under the constant assault of weight-based discrimination, or any form of discrimination for that matter, can shorten your lifespan.[192]

So what can be done to set the workplace straight on weight-based discrimination? We've condensed the excellent recommendations from the November 2020 *Obesity Stigma at Work* report by Purpose below, but to read the report in further detail, you can find it on the Employment Studies website.[193]

Facing Anti-fatness in the Workplace:

1. **Hold your workplace accountable.** Company equality, diversity and inclusion policies, and anti-discrimination training should include weight-based discrimination. Any dress codes or appearance-based standards for employees should not directly or indirectly discriminate against employees based on weight. If your workplace implements health and well-being practices, they should support, not stigmatize, fat employees.
2. **Find an advocate.** If you feel you're being discriminated against, make sure you have support to help you navigate your employer's policies or employment law. You may want to start the process informally by speaking with

your manager, a member of your HR team, or a union representative, or even run it past a trusted colleague.

3. **Know your rights.** If you've been unsuccessful in resolving your issues informally and want to escalate things, it's a good idea to engage with a third party such as your union official; Advisory, Conciliation and Arbitration Service (ACAS); Citizen's Advice; etc. These organizations are best placed to advise on what you'll need in order to advance your grievance and also assist you with keeping your relationship with your employer and coworkers as uncontentious as possible.

4. **Be an active self-manager.** This is key for anyone going through a reporting process at work: keep a close eye on your mood and the levels of stress and fatigue you are feeling. Watch for potential patterns and get information from your health partner on how you can minimize the impact of the above triggers on your mental health and overall well-being. This is especially important if you have health conditions related to your weight.

Unsurprisingly, what disabled people, particularly disabled women, face in the workplace and the wider world is also profoundly inequitable. Roughly one in ten working women has a disability, which can be paralysis, chronic pain and illness, impaired hearing or vision, learning disabilities, and mental health diagnoses.[194] The UN estimates that 75 percent of disabled women are unemployed and, when employed, earn less than disabled men and non-disabled women.[195] In the UK, the average pay gap for disabled women, compared to the average earnings of non-disabled men, is 36 percent less, equivalent to £3.68 less per hour.[196] In the US, disabled women earn seventy-two cents for every dollar earned by disabled men, and a report by the American Association of University Women found disabled people made sixty-eight cents for every dollar earned by non-disabled people.[197] When different lenses of discrimination are applied, like systemic racism and queer- or transphobia, the inequity disabled women face is further exacerbated.[198] In the US, some disabled people are legally allowed to be paid as little as twenty-two cents an hour because of Section 14(c) of the Fair Labor Standards Act, which allows employers to pay disabled people below the minimum wage simply by obtaining a certificate from the Department of Labor.[199]

Within an ableist structure of the traditional workplace, the overarching experiences of disabled people, particularly disabled women, are dire. Studies show that disabled women are more likely to be interrupted, tone policed (i.e. told they are being too angry, emotional, etc.), have their judgment called into question, and are less likely to feel appreciated and supported by their companies than their non-disabled colleagues.[200] A quarter of disabled women surveyed reported that they were given the same opportunities for advancement as their non-disabled colleagues. Over 50 percent of disabled women surveyed said they were often or always burned out and consistently felt exhausted. Because of this, disabled women are more likely to be considering leaving their jobs than their non-disabled colleagues.

You would think that the recent drive for diversity and inclusion in the corporate world would push companies to take accessibility and disability awareness more seriously. Unfortunately, a recent study showed that company-wide disability awareness and equality measures are being prioritized only 25 percent of the time, a paltry figure compared to the 40 percent afforded to gender identity and sexual orientation and the 60 percent afforded to race and ethnicity.[201]This is especially apparent regarding workplace harassment, which indicates that perceived power differential between disabled and non-disabled people.

In the corporate world, disabled women experience multiple forms of harassment, with 54 percent of disabled women surveyed by TUC reported experiencing two or more different types of sexually harassing behavior,[202] which more often than not goes unreported. Sixy-six percent of the disabled women surveyed who had experienced sexual harassment at work didn't report it due to fears it wouldn't be taken seriously, or would negatively impact their career trajectory. When disabled women did report sexual harassment, 53 percent said it wasn't dealt with appropriately by their company. The experience of sexual harassment negatively affected the mental health of 34 percent of the disabled women surveyed, with 12 percent of those women saying their experiences forced them to leave their employers.[203]

When you consider the above statistics and add on the fact that disabled women and girls are twice as likely as non-disabled women and girls to experience gender-based violence, and that disabled women are often denied access to reproductive health care and can still be subjected to forced sterilization in thirty-four US states,[204] it's not hard to understand the immense stress disabled women must shoulder every day. Discrimination against disabled women in the workplace and the world erodes the idea of democracy and is a severe hindrance to national economic development and innovation.

This issue is much larger and more nuanced than we could ever do justice to here, not least because we are not the right people to educate others about disability rights and advocacy. We have brought to your attention this important issue in the hope that you will educate yourself further. If you hold a position within your company where you can influence change, we hope you'll take the following advice we've gleaned from The Partnership on Employment & Accessible Technology (PEAT):

1. Your hiring process should be accessible: use closed captioning, ensure adequate screen contrast, remove time restrictions on applications, and ensure your applications are compatible with screen readers.

2. Offer all positions as flexible or part-time, unless there is a justifiable business reason not to.
3. Your workplace should be physcially accessible: provide ramps in addition to stairs; provide accessible and/or ambulant toilet and shower facilities; provide hearing loops, adjustable desks, and assistive platforms.
4. Your workplace should be technologically accessible: have refreshable Braille displays, use sign language and speech recognition apps, and offer color-coded keypads.

This list is not exhaustive, and we are not disability educators. The best way to ensure your company is accessible to disabled people is to hire a disability educator to help shape your accessibility policies.

No matter what you face in the workplace, you will always need to be your own advocate. The amount of time we've wasted waiting for someone to notice our suffering (or excellence) and speak up on our behalf is beyond measure. You need to recognize and value your skill set, your time, your intellect, and ultimately, yourself, because there will always be people in the workplace, and the wider world, who will treat you appallingly if you let them. Bearing in mind that women in the workplace who openly appreciate themselves also have targets on their backs, we'd much rather that you faced the discriminatory practices of the corporate world knowing how much you bring to the table rather than feeling like you're never enough.

So how can we get ourselves to a place where we're feeling balanced and strong enough to loudly love ourselves in the workplace? Here's what works for us (most of the time).

"Bitch, You Doin' a Good Job" – Destini Ann:

- **Recognize your triggers.** As you move through life, you accumulate and (hopefully) heal trauma. This trauma informs your boundaries. You need to understand what your boundaries are and where they lie, so you'll know when they're being crossed. Feeling triggered (instantly angry, sad, scared) is a strong indication that your boundaries are being threatened or crossed. Knowing your boundaries, like engaging in self-care, is not a one-off thing. It's a dynamic, evolving process. Regular self-check-in will help strengthen the bond between your head and body so that you'll be much more aware when someone is getting on your last nerve, long before that nerve starts to fray. We cannot say enough how important it is not to lose your shit and waste precious energy on someone who doesn't deserve your attention or time. Save your emotions for the people, places, and experiences that truly deserve them.
- **Regular self-care is nonnegotiable.** We're saying it again. This is not taking care of basic human needs for sleep, food, and general cleanliness. This is not a "one and done" kind of thing. We're talking about making regularly occurring space to reconnect your mind and body, to engage in activities that light your inner fire, to rest deeply (follow the Nap Ministry on Instagram for more on this), and to chase joy in whatever form it takes. How often does this happen for you? Being totally honest, our joy landscape has been pretty barren for the last few years, and we're having to make a concerted effort to not feel guilty when we take time out for ourselves, to not succumb to the lie that we don't have time to invest in ourselves. We always have time. We have just chosen for too long to invest that time in those around us instead of in ourselves. Choosing yourself does not mean that those

around you don't matter. It means that you're aware enough to realize that only when your cup is filled are you in a balanced, healthy place to fill up others.

- **Move your body.** This doesn't mean run a marathon or complete a triathlon, although if you feel moved to do so, by all means, please do. We know that when you move your body, however you're able to, it sends a message to the reward centers of your brain to release chemicals like dopamine, which help you feel pleasure, motivation, and hope. The more you engage in regular body movement, the more dopamine receptors and circulating dopamine you have in your brain.[205] Moving your body is directly connected to feeling happiness and hope, two things women desperately need as they navigate the workplace and the wider world.

- **Celebrate every milestone.** The word "celebrate" comes from the Latin word "celebrare": assemble to honor. Learn to celebrate everything, from the little triumphs to the huge achievements. Don't treat any of your accomplishments as unimportant or unworthy of recognition. Down that road lies unending dissatisfaction and a feeling of unfulfillment. It's the story of the person who always dreamed of owning a Porsche and, when they were finally able to afford one, were disappointed that they couldn't afford a Maserati. If you only value money, accolades, and promotions, nothing will ever be enough as there will always be someone else with more money, more accolades, and a bigger title. Money comes and goes; accolades and promotions are subjective; but when you view your career path with incremental, dynamic growth as the objective, you will always find something to celebrate.

To learn more, please check out these additional resources:

Books

- Gordon, Aubrey. *What We Don't Talk about When We Talk about Fat.* Boston: Beacon Press, 2020.
- Pinder-Amaker, Stephanie, and Lauren Wadsworth. *Did That Just Happen?!: Beyond "Diversity"—Creating Sustainable and Inclusive Organizations.* Boston: Beacon Press, 2021.

Activists/ Influencers

- Andrew Gurza (they/he)
  - Instagram @andrewgurza1
  - www.andrewgurza.com
  - Podcast: Disability After Dark
- Aubrey Gordon *she/her*
  - Instagram @yrfatfriend
  - www.yourfatfriend.com
- Diets Don't Work (Debbie *she/her*)
  - Instagram @diets_dont_work_haes1
  - www.diets-dont-work.net
- Imani Barbarin (she/her)
  - Instagram @crutches_and_spice
  - Tiktok @crutches_and_spice
- The Body is Not an Apology
  - Instagram @thebodyisnotanapology
  - www.SonyaReneeTaylor.com
- The Nap Ministry
  - Instagram @thenapministry
  - www.thenapministry.wordpress.com

- Upgrade Accessibility
  - Instagram @upgradeaccessibility
  - www.upgradeaccessibility.com
  - Podcast: The Politics of Disability
- Victoria *she/they*
  - Instagram @fatfabfeminist
  - TikTok @fatfabfeminist

CHAPTER 12
BURN OUT ISN'T (YOUR) FAILURE

The most common way people give up their power
is by thinking they don't have any.
—ALICE WALKER

Lisa's Story:

had just returned to work after having my son and taking nearly a year of maternity leave. I was working from home two days a week and commuting into London the other three. I'd been given two new projects, fast-paced but small builds, which would have been no problem for me just a year before. Now I couldn't seem to keep my personal life and my work life in balance. When I was with my son, I obsessively checked my phone for emails, calls, and texts, stressing myself out about how much work I hadn't gotten done that day. When I was in the office, I was initially happy to have my own space and would work efficiently for the first few hours before an insidious feeling of guilt would start to creep in. Was my son okay? Was he missing me and crying incessantly? Was my "selfish" need to pursue a career going to emotionally fuck him up? No part of my life felt right. When I was at home, I couldn't leave my work alone, and I felt like I wasn't giving enough *of myself to my son. When I was at work, I tortured myself about how shit I was as a mother and imagined terrible things happening to my son. It doesn't take a genius to see that this wasn't heading anywhere good.*

I had had severe stomach pain for over a month before I finally made time to see my doctor, who ran tests and found a bacterial infection in my stomach. She prescribed a short dose of antibiotics, which I immediately picked up from the pharmacy, so I could start my first dose that evening. I needed to get better ASAP; so much work to do!

The next morning, I woke up awash with pain. I could barely move my head from one side to the other, my lower back screamed, and I walked slowly down the stairs with a limp as I couldn't put all my weight onto my right foot. I had gone to bed a fairly fit (but severely stressed) thirty-five-year-old and woken up feeling like I was on my deathbed. I thought I'd just slept in a bad position, took the strongest pain medication I could find, and gingerly got myself ready for work and my son ready for his day as my partner had already left. I don't remember much about that day at work or the rest of that week, as it's obscured by a fog of pain. I crept around the office like a ghost, I crawled up and down the stairs, I was unable to lift my son, and each day I woke up with more parts of my body aching.

After three days of escalating pain, I called my doctor and begged to come in. When I sat down with her a few hours later, I tried to explain the pain that was radiating from my fingers and toes, into my wrists and ankles, down my neck, and into my lower back, running from hip joint to hip joint. She was stunned by the change and ran multiple tests on me to try and understand what was causing this sudden and widespread pain. She put me onto a short course of high dosage steroids, thinking the pain might be caused by inflammation and hoping it would control my symptoms. The steroids worked immediately, knocking out all of the pain, though

I could still feel something in the areas where the pain had been, like pressure or tension.

When my course of steroids ended, the pain came back almost immediately and proliferated. Each morning there was a new part of my body that felt inflamed and couldn't be touched. I was sleeping for an hour or two at a time before waking in pain. My test results came back and showed no sign of any inflammation; whatever was causing this pain wasn't readily detectable, and all my doctor could do was send me for more tests and put me back on steroids. She warned me that I couldn't stay on steroids indefinitely—there would be too much damage done to my bones and internal organs. When I asked her what she thought it might be, she said it could be seronegative rheumatoid arthritis or fibromyalgia, but without getting some kind of definitive test result, she couldn't give me a diagnosis that would help me find a permanent solution for the pain. I stayed on steroids for another month; the additional testing came back showing nothing, just like the first round, and I was taken off steroids for the second time.

Again, the pain came back almost immediately, and my doctor referred me to a rheumatologist who I was luckily able to see quickly. He asked countless questions about the pain, how it started, what it felt like, where it was, and more tests were done. I was put back on an even higher dose of steroids so that the rheumatologist could understand how quickly the pain came back as I was weaned off. At the end of two months, I was back to feeling all of the pain, but the rheumatologist was no closer to diagnosing me.

While all of this was going on, I had left my old job for a new one that had promised me flexibility and a healthy work-life balance, and ended up being the complete opposite. I was working twelve-hour days, running around London on minimal sleep, amped to the whites of my eyes on steroids, seeing my son for an hour each day (my partner had pretty much taken over his complete care), and driving myself deeper into the ground.

I remember watching the rheumatologist look through the thick sheaf of test results and various scans of my joints that showed no inflammation anywhere, and his look of confusion said it all: what was going on? He reiterated what my doctor had said: I couldn't stay on the steroids any longer. He believed there might be a problem with my immune system, and it needed to be reset; he asked if I was willing to start a course of immunosuppressants and handed me pamphlets for the drugs he was recommending. He asked me to read through them and call his office on Monday morning (it was a Friday) to let them know I was ready to start the treatment. I walked down the hallway reading through the pamphlets for these drugs, commonly used for chemotherapy and only to be used for severe conditions due to the seriousness of their potential side effects. Reading those words drove home that what was happening to me was serious; it hit me like an anvil, the comedy piano squashing me into the ground. I don't think I slept more than a few hours that night.

Deep down, I couldn't believe that this was all necessary, that the "turn it off and turn it on again" approach for my immune system was the only option. No one had asked me about my stress levels or my workload; no one had asked me about how much sleep I was getting; and no one asked me how much I was drinking. But I knew, and I knew it wasn't right: my life had gone from slightly imbalanced to completely unstable, and I hadn't done a single thing to make it better. I didn't get much continuous sleep at night anyway (hello, toddler!), so I drank shitloads of caffeine during the day, which kept my adrenal system cranked to the max. I didn't make time to eat regularly during the day, so I put my body into starvation mode and crashed with fatigue when I got home, which meant I was too tired to exercise, and my mental health nosedived even further. I had at least two stiff drinks a night to relax because it was a quick fix, even though it tended to make me feel depressed the next day and caused sleep disturbances even on the nights when my son did sleep all the way through. I was the perfect embodiment of a rat on a treadmill: running myself to nowhere, for no good reason, and ruining my health in the process.

Getting to this stage was the best thing that could have ever happened to me. It forced me to stop and realize how I was an active participant in my own burnout. Perhaps subconsciously, I was doing it because I knew I couldn't be the kind of woman (mother, partner, sister, daughter, friend) that I wanted to be while I continued to pursue this kind of lifestyle. I had to call it.

That weekend, I decided to stop all the unhealthy behaviors. First, I quit my job and found one that was more on board with what my work-life balance needed to be. I had come across a few studies that demonstrated real turnaround in inflammation and pain levels on a plant-based diet, so I went vegan that weekend, and haven't looked back. I also took a hard look at what alcohol was giving to my life and what it was taking away; the answer was that it took more than it gave, and what it was giving, I could get from exercise. So I recommitted to making exercise a regular part of my life, and alcohol became a weekend benefit, not a nightly necessity. The joint pain still crops up from time to time, always when I'm stressed and running myself down, but it quickly fades once I go back to giving my body what it needs: rest, hydration, nutritious food, regular exercise, and kindness. Kindness, something I value highly, was a missing piece in my life, along with forgiveness, acceptance of who I am, and the grace of knowing that if I continue to make myself a priority, I will continue to get better.

You know that feeling you get halfway through Sunday afternoon, when you start to feel anxious or easily annoyed? You can't believe the weekend went so fast—where did Saturday go? That feeling continues all night, maybe wakes you up a few times, and each time you wake, there's a sense of impending doom. Then, painfully, it's the morning, and you get yourself ready; maybe you have to get children ready as well, help a partner, or perhaps you're a caretaker for a family member and need to take care of them before you can leave the house. The whole time you're doing this, all you can think is, "I don't want to go. I don't want to waste my whole day, my whole life, at this job." You walk, cycle, take a train, car, or bus—however you get to work, the whole journey is spent under a dark cloud, a ball of anxiety growing in the pit of your stomach. It tells you that everything you are about to do is wrong. It makes your head ache, shoulders hunch, and teeth clench. Welcome to burnout.

Here's a question: Do you love, or even like, your job? Does your job cause you to feel stress and/or anxiety constantly? If it does, is your job worth the pain? Maybe you've answered "yes" to this last one, but we're not quite finished.

Do you have young children? Do you have a child with special needs? Are you a single parent? Are you isolated and without a support system or family members close by? Are you a caretaker to other family members? Is it worthwhile for you to have a job that creates feelings of stress and anxiety while you try to balance the needs and desires of your complex personal life? If you're still answering with a strong yes, then you're committed to the struggle, and we respect your decision. We also fully recognize that there will be points in your life where making big changes will be financially impossible, specifically if you are a single parent, on a low income, or have complex care duties. If, however, your "yes" is wavering, or it's only there because you feel you have literally no choice other than to remain at this job to keep your head above water, please hear us out.

How you structure your life balance is no one's decision but yours; however, some semblance of balance has to be maintained between our personal lives and our professional ambitions if we want to make it work long-term. Just as you cannot physically work two full-time jobs (and live to tell the tale), you cannot stack yourself out daily with both tasks and mental load. It is simply not sustainable. You may have been raised to be a "yes girl" where no day is ever too busy for you to not take on more work if required, but you're setting a dangerous precedent that you will always be expected to achieve and feel pulled to surpass.

There is no shame in admitting when you've taken on more responsibilities than one person can possibly hold. Coming from a healthy place of balance, being a full-time caretaker, and having a paid full-time job would not be achievable. Being the primary or sole caretaker for a child or adult with specialized care needs would not be compatible with having a paid full-time job. Having children, working a full-time job, and having a side hustle is not something you can sustain long-term—believe us when we say this, as unpopular an opinion as it may be! These statements might seem obvious to some, but they need to be said as there is a pervasive delusion going around misleading women into thinking that they can balance any amount of responsibility that gets placed on their shoulders. We already know that women bear 70 percent of the global unpaid care burden, and that women are eight times more likely than their male partners to stay home from work with a sick child[206]—do we really need to add more tasks to our to-do lists when so many of us are already drowning?

When you work in the corporate world, which is founded on patriarchal principles, there is no doubt that leaving "early" to pick your kids up from school or having to stay home with sick children impacts how you are perceived in your workplace. No one ever questions why children's school hours and adult's working hours don't dovetail, there is only the levying of career penalties on those mothers who have the audacity to want to work outside the home. The stress and expectation rests heavily on our shoulders, and all too often it leads to women switching to a job with better flexibility or the ability to work from home, many of which are lower paid and negatively impact both career trajectory and lifetime earnings, which in turn affect retirement and pension funds.

According to a 2018 Merrill Lynch study, a woman's lifetime earnings can potentially be as much as $1,055,000 less than a man's when pay gap data is included with the typically female work-life interruptions of taking time off to have children, working flexibly, and caring for elderly family members.[207] It should come as no surprise that women are more likely to stop working to look after elderly family members than their male partners, in part because women tend to make less than men (due to the work-life interruptions detailed above) but also because it is a societal expectation of women that they take on care roles.

One of our mother's friends always says, "I can do anything for six weeks," which has been our mantra for years. For six weeks, we can survive a pervy boss, make our lives work on shit pay, deal with belittling colleagues, and ignore harassment until something better comes along. The problem with this kind of thinking is that we continually find ourselves running our mental health, and subsequently our physical health, into the ground. Even if that only happens for six weeks, which is generally not the case, women do not get cared for the way men do. If you're in a cis-het relationship as a woman, the odds are that there won't be someone at the end of the day asking you how your emotional balance is, allowing you to vent about your day, and doing their part in the cooking, cleaning, and childcare (if you've got kids). Your pattern is more likely to be that after a long day of paid work, you walk in the door to someone else who needs feeding and/or care, a house that needs cleaning, clothes that need washing, and you probably still have leftover work from your paid job looming overhead. Your workday extends on and on because there are meals to cook, people to care for, and things to clean up before you can even begin to care for yourself. Even engaging in self-care can seem like a mountain of work: we're sold every possible concoction to keep our skin looking like that of an eighteen-year-old. If we've had a baby, we need to exercise until we look better than we did before we got pregnant. It isn't enough for us to care for our families and nurture our careers. We also carry the weight of society's expectations of what we should look like, how much we should weigh, that we dress stylishly, and that we always are kind, smiling, and happy.

But we digress. Society tells women that they can achieve any kind of work-life balance they dream up. Want to study all night for a new degree and work all day at your full-time job? Why not! Want to work a sixty-hour week and then spend the weekend chasing up your "side hustle"? Of course you can! There are twenty-four usable hours in the day. How much sleep do you really need? Martha Stewart went on record claiming to only sleep four hours a night[208]—the message being that if you want to achieve great things, don't waste time sleeping. The problem is that we don't all have the immense wealth and privilege of Martha Stewart, and, let's be honest, not even Martha Stewart can survive long-term on four hours of sleep a night. Studies show that people who consistently sleep less than seven hours a night are at a much higher risk of developing chronic conditions like depression, cardiovascular disease, and diabetes.[209] Women, in particular, are sensitive to lack of sleep as it impacts the endocrine system, which governs our hormones, and our bodies are continually passing through phases of hormonal change. When we put ourselves under immense strain with the life choices we are making, and perhaps feel forced to make in order to *have it all*, our physical and mental health seriously suffers. At some point, you have to acknowledge that you cannot do everything and know that admitting this is *not* a failure, just an acceptance of reality. When you can get to this point of honesty, only then can you take a step back and evaluate with clear eyes what kind of pressures you are under and whether they are worth the pain.

Our friends without children often ask us if having children is "worth it." For us, we feel that having children *is* worth it, but it's definitely not easy. Having children is incredibly hard, not least because your body has to internally rearrange itself to make room for that baby. Then you have to get that baby out, and no matter how you do it, there is blood, pain, and healing required. At that point, however, you have a newborn, so you don't have time to heal. You fall headfirst into an ongoing series of cat naps that make you feel even more tired than you did when you fell asleep. At the same time, your hormones completely desert you, and you literally can't stop crying, all to the soundtrack of a hungry baby's wail. Babies fall into sleep patterns and then suddenly stop sleeping again, which goes on for a really long time. We're talking years, not months. They get weaned onto solid food and start to eat everything, only to become toddlers who hate everything but one specific, totally unhealthy food. They find out they can say "no" to you, and they practice this for years, peaking in their teens when they perfect slamming doors, dramatic sighs, and repeatedly assuring you that you're a huge embarrassment and always have been.

There is also the undeniable fact that having children makes your paid work life harder. You may need to work flexibly, which means you'll tend to get paid less and may be passed up for promotions, you probably won't be able to attend last-minute meetings or work events, and when your child is sick it will probably be you who needs to stay home. As we discussed in chapter 8, you as a woman will pay for this decision, but all things considered, we still think that having children has been the most amazing, life-altering decision we ever made, and we wouldn't give it up. For us, this is a pressure worth having, but not every woman needs it or wants it in their life.

What are your pressures? Are they worth it?

In the first six months of our podcast *Dear Patriarchy*, we covered burnout at least three times. In all honesty, most of the topics we discuss come back to the burned-out baseline most women operate from. The vast majority of women are running with an empty tank, trying to fill others from a cup that is bone dry. And guess what?

It's not their fault. Women are presented with an unending list of tasks and expectations. The Patriarchy begins heaping them on us when we're young girls. Take your doll and practice running a house. Take your play kitchen and get all geared up for years of making mac and cheese and fish sticks.

Women and girls are expected to be perfect. We are conditioned to be prim, proper, and perfectly poised. Keep a pristine house, snag a man, maintain a happy household, have children. Host perfectly pinnable birthday parties, Instagram-worthy meals, picturesque holidays, crafty gifts for teachers and friends, and a nice tight ass. Gotta get those workouts in, ladies!

Fuck. That. Noise.

None of it is real. We spoke in chapter 8 about striving for a "good enough" life. It is up to you to reframe your life and expectations. There are lists that float around social media from time to time saying what a woman should get rid of to be perfect. There are countless versions, ranging from leaving behind your "nasty side," your fears, or the excess weight you gained on vacation five years ago and never got around to losing. Let us just say that the only thing a woman needs to shed is the weight of other people's expectations. In Lisa's story at the start of the chapter, we saw a woman running herself ragged to achieve something, to chase a dream. But threaded throughout her story are the weight and expectations from society, coworkers, bosses, and that things should all work out a certain way. No one is living your life. No one knows the manifold moving parts of your life like you do, so no one but you can ultimately decide what's right, or wrong, for you. Setting boundaries is an important following action once you've decided what works, or doesn't work, for you. When stresses start to pile up, you need to identify when there's too much going on and delegate, refuse, cancel, and create space for yourself to rest. No one will do it for you because no one *can* do it for you.

If you are facing burnout and you're drowning under the weight of it, we feel for you; we have been there and are, very likely, still there at this very moment in one way or the other. We are all burned out. We are all either at our breaking points, or just about to hit that motherfucker like a ten-ton truck. While we can't help pull you out of the hole, we can encourage you to take small steps now to help extricate yourself from the darkness. Start to create space and light for yourself in a joyous place where you have firm boundaries and a clear, intentional plan. Make the decision today to start the journey to a healthier, happier, more fulfilled you.

How to Blast through Burnout Fog & Refill Your Cup:

- Drink water and eat nourishing whole foods.
- Identify impossible tasks and other mental load items.
- Prioritize, delegate, or dismiss things not worth your time and energy.
- Make space for yourself to have time alone or in silence.
- Say no to plans or projects that fill you with dread. Our mantra is, if it's not a "hell yes," it's a "no."
- Move your beautiful body.
- Spend time in loose, breathable clothing (or in the buff).
- Be kind to yourself. Cut out negative self-talk or guilt from others' expectations.
- Extricate yourself from toxic people, places, things, or situations.
- Stop caring about people or things that no longer enrich your life. It's okay to say goodbye.

To learn more, please check out these additional resources:

Books

- Nagoski, Emily, and Amelia Nagoski. *Burnout: The Secret to Unlocking the Stress Cycle.* New York: Ballantine Books, 2019.
- Schuster, Tara. *Buy Yourself the F*cking Lilies: And Other Rituals to Fix Your Life, from Someone Who's Been There.* New York: Dial Press, 2019.
- Knight, Sara. *The Life-Changing Magic of Not Giving a F*ck: How to Stop Spending Time You Don't Have with People You Don't Like Doing Things You Don't Want to Do (A No F*cks Given Guide).* New York: Little, Brown and Company, 2015.

CHAPTER 13
SHECESSION

*I am not free while any woman is unfree, even when
her shackles are very different from my own.*
—AUDRE LORDE

When our global understanding of a "normal" life evaporated
in early 2020, everyone held their breath to see what our
new reality would be when this history-making, world-
stopping pandemic was finally over. Two years on, we can see that
the pandemic won't be over any time soon, and we'll probably
spend the next few years getting populations under control as
new variants flare and spike around the globe. As offices started
to reopen at the end of 2020 and people began to return to the
workforce, news outlets began to report that women were leaving,
or being forcibly ejected from, the workforce *en masse*. Because it
was a phenomenon that disproportionately impacted women, the
media felt compelled to give it a quirky, cute name. Did they do that
to make it more easily dismissible or to make it easier to shift the
responsibility for resolving it from those in positions of power onto
those directly affected by it? Whatever the reason, this massive shift
of women out of the workforce was dubbed the "shecession."[210]

As the world shut down, country by country, we watched the same thing happen to working women. While they joined their colleagues in the struggle to figure out how to effectively and efficiently work remotely, working women also took on increased domestic responsibility and unpaid care work. Mothers became full-time teachers, cooks, and cleaners while also shouldering the majority of the burden of all the other domestic tasks that keep a home and family running. Mothers who also worked outside the home did all of the above while trying to keep their kids from gate-crashing virtual work meetings. All of a sudden, the delicate balance of work and home was laid bare for everyone to see. The true, ongoing struggle for equilibrium by working women and mothers who chose to work outside the home was brought to light. And it all came crashing down.

Globally, 114 million jobs were lost in 2020, and women experienced 5 percent employment loss—approximately 64 million jobs—to men's 3.9 percent. This represented a global earning loss for women of at least $800 million, more than the combined GDP of ninety-eight countries.[211]

When Deloitte polled over 5,000 women across ten countries, only 22 percent of women believed that their employers allowed them to set clear boundaries between their work lives and personal lives. Seventy-seven percent of the women polled said that their workloads had increased during the pandemic, while 66 percent held the greatest responsibility for domestic tasks, and 59 percent reported spending increased time each day completing domestic tasks. Mothers were three times as likely as fathers to be responsible for domestic tasks and care work and twice as likely to worry about their work performance being negatively judged because of their increased care requirements. Interestingly, more than 70 percent of fathers polled thought they were splitting the household chores equally, but only 44 percent of mothers felt that was the case. On average, nearly half of the women polled had to modify their working hours in order to cover their increased care responsibilities and experienced a negative impact on their relationships with their employers because of it. More than half of the Black women and women of Color polled experienced this, and 65 percent of the single mothers polled reported this as well.[212]

In addition to feeling increased negativity about their career prospects, women were also feeling more unsafe at work than ever before. During the pandemic, 52 percent of the women polled by Deloitte were subjected to harassment or microaggressions of some kind, ranging from their judgment being publicly called into question; to experiencing sexual harassment; to receiving discriminatory, disparaging comments from their male colleagues. Unsurprisingly, many of these incidents went unreported as the women affected feared having a career penalty of some kind levied against them as a result of reporting a colleague.[213]

As if that wasn't enough, 42 percent of the total women polled said their career paths weren't progressing as they had hoped; 52 percent of the Black women and women of Color reported experiencing this. Fifty-one percent of women said they felt less optimistic about their career opportunities and trajectories than they did pre-pandemic. This left 57 percent of the women polled planning to leave their jobs within the next two years, 21 percent of them in less than a year. Poor mental health along with poor work-life balance were key reasons behind women's dissatisfaction with their career trajectories and their current employers.[214]

We already knew that women would be dealt a heavy blow if the requirement for unpaid care work increased, and unsurprisingly, the impact of COVID-19 has specifically and disproportionately targeted Black women and women of Color. Even before the pandemic hit, for every one hundred men promoted to manager, only fifty-eight Black women and seventy-one Latinas were promoted. Once the pandemic began, Black women and women of Color were more likely to be laid off or furloughed, presenting even further barriers to advancement on top of those that were already present. When you add to this the concentrated impact of COVID-19 on Black communities and communities of Color, as well as the heavy and ever-increasing emotional load of racial violence on the Black community, particularly in America, the exponential increase of inequity since 2020 is heart-rending and cannot be ignored within the corporate world.[215]

Flash forward to December 2020, and many people seemed to conveniently forget about the extra weight that had been loaded onto women's shoulders worldwide. Media pundits and government officials bemoaned the fact that there was no one to do all the paid work that was going undone, and we say to this: where was the support for working women? Where was the infrastructure? Who is going to lift or lighten the heavy domestic load women carry? The truth of the matter was, is, and always will be that there is a lack of infrastructure to support women in the workforce because women's labor is not valued in the same way as men's labor. Necessary things like affordable, easily accessible childcare settings and efficient, low-cost transportation systems benefit all women, whether they're single or partnered, with kids or without. It's difficult for women to survive and thrive in the corporate world because it wasn't built for us, and our labor is routinely treated as secondary or unimportant, at least until the global economy grinds to a halt under the weight of a worldwide pandemic.

Around the globe, women are disproportionately represented in jobs that pay low wages, offer few benefits, and are the least secure. In the United States, those working in the high-stress, low-pay retail and hospitality industries are predominantly women, and they're the industries most directly impacted by the COVID-19 crisis. Of the forty lowest-paying industries, which employ over twenty-two million people in America alone, women make up 64 percent of the workforce.[216]

We've said it many times before, and we'll continue to say it until it sticks: the term "unskilled labor" is a misnomer. Jobs that entail "unskilled labor work" are made up of hard, often grueling work that typically involves painfully repetitive tasks. The predominant population of the unskilled labor force is single mothers, though conservative politicians would have you believe it's made up of twenty-something stoners sitting on their couches, not wanting to work because they make more money on unemployment. In reality, during the pandemic, American families were brutally impacted by the increased cost of living and the lack of a national living wage while more than a third of the UK's poorest families spent more than ever before on food, gas, and electricity. And now we see a mass exodus of women leaving the workforce, not because they want to, but because they had to. Why? Because with school and childcare settings closed, the key infrastructure mothers who work outside the home need to support their careers disappeared. The bottom fell out, and women just couldn't make it work anymore. Another reason is because there's no money. Women who lost their jobs, were made redundant, furloughed, or otherwise lost their ability to earn, now can't afford to put their kids in care settings or extracurricular programs. Government aid has been a welcome help, but even at its most plentiful, the amount paid out is insufficient to cover the high cost of childcare, which was exorbitant pre-pandemic and will undoubtedly become even harder to secure due to a reduced amount of settings affording fewer available places.

The impact of the pandemic on people with disabilities has been monumental, specifically for women with disabilities. While remote and flexible working—something disability advocates have been requesting for decades to support disabled people in the corporate world—have been key to safeguarding their wellbeing and safety, women with disabilities were more worried about the potential negative career impact than non-disabled women. Disabled women were twice as likely to say that setting boundaries with their employers, regarding availability or having mental breaks, has negatively impacted their careers over the last year. Disabled women were also more likely to feel judged for requesting remote working or flexible hours and, as more disabled women said their career stagnated in the last year than non-disabled women, it is a valid concern.[217]

All of this and we haven't even touched on the rates of domestic and sexual violence, which skyrocketed during lockdown as women and children were trapped with their abusers or whose unstable home lives left them at the mercy of predatory men. In the UK, from April to June of 2020, there was a 65 percent increase in calls to the National Domestic Abuse Helpline compared with the amount of calls made from January to March 2020.[218] Across the globe, instances of domestic violence (DV) soared when national lockdowns were initiated: a 30 percent rise in France and 25 percent rise in Argentina from their March 2020 lockdowns, an 8.1 percent rise in the US (though researchers expect the real figure is much higher) and a tripling of DV in China's Hubei region from February 2020. Calls to helplines in Cyprus and Singapore jumped 30 and 33 percent respectively from the start of their March 2020 lockdowns.[219] With the closure of schools around the globe, many permanently, the lack of educational opportunities will impact girls tremendously. UNESCO estimates that eleven million girls worldwide are at risk of not returning to school once the pandemic finally subsides, putting them at increased risk of teenage pregnancy, early or forced marriage, and acts of violence.[220]

The impact of COVID-19 on the world has been far-reaching, but on women and girls, it will be life-changing for generations to come if governments don't act now to protect the strides we had made leading up to the pandemic in engendering equality in the workplace, the schoolroom, and the wider world. The World Economic Forum's *2021 Global Gender Gap* report posits that gender equality has been set back by at least ten years by the onset of COVID-19. The report also states that if we remain at our current trajectory, it will take 135.6 years to close the global gender pay gap.[221]

And so we look again at the shecession, with its cutesy, imbecilic title. It is, in fact, a deeply unjust reverberation of the global pandemic which, at the time of writing, has killed 6.34 million people and has swiftly turned the tide of women's enfranchisement, not just in the corporate environment, but in the classroom, on the streets, and around the world. It has demolished the lifelong dedication of millions of women over the last century (and beyond) to prove their worth, their ability, and the strength of their character under the incessant and oppressive onslaught of the Patriarchy.

CONCLUSION
HOW IT STARTED ... HOW IT'S GOING

*At the end of the day, we can endure much
more than we think we can.*
–FRIDA KAHLO

When we started the work that would become this book early in 2018, neither one of us realized the tremendous weight of the experiences we were carrying. We had always had the shared dream of becoming published authors and the goal of writing a book, but making the decision to begin this venture together, to write out our experiences—we weren't ready for the heaviness of it, the heart-wrenching pain of hearing each other's terrible stories and being forced to look at the experiences we shared in common with fresh eyes.

The incredible thing is that once the gaslighting has stopped and the hot air is let out of the room, all that's left is the memory of the trauma and whatever emotions you used to protect yourself so that you could move forward. Looking back and clearly seeing all the things that happened to us over the years is horrifying. Hearing the echoes of the terrible things that were said to us against the stark background we can now identify as the Patriarchy, realizing we were constantly absorbing brutal misogyny and blaming ourselves for it, is mind-blowing. We had been carrying the guilt of alienating "well-meaning" women who, upon closer inspection, were actually protecting the very people whose boots were on not just our necks, but theirs as well. These women, self-appointed protectors of the Patriarchy, were being lied to, held back, and disqualified from roles that they should have been awarded decades before. Hearing their bullshit justification as they tried to convince themselves as well as us that we were all so lucky to have jobs that robbed us of our drive and ambition. Letting them talk us out of reporting incidents that broke multiple laws, letting their flimsy words make us feel like we were what was broken, that we were the problem. The abuse we hid and absorbed while we were "put in our place" by people, mainly men but sometimes women, whom we truly hoped were building us up, mentoring us. The stark reality of the gaslighting, inequity, and discrimination that had shredded us to shadows, as we continued to show up and persevere only to be transferred, let go, or simply ignored until we quit, became very real.

And now, this work has become our life's passion. Through this work, we faced the reality of what was done to us, time and again, by faceless corporations and by countless managers, some of whom specifically told us they wanted to screw us and others who just did it with their disrespect and carelessness. Through mountains of research, pages of statistics, and endless anecdotes from our podcast listeners and the incredible community we are building on social media, we know that we aren't alone and that our work is valid—not least because we are going through this together, with a group of strong, determined women, many of whom have been to hell and back.

The plight of the working woman is heavily chronicled, condemned, praised, and ultimately, belittled. We get told every day, through a multitude of almost imperceptible microaggressions, how we are supposed to feel about ourselves and others like us. So we wanted to make sure we approached this book with love and open hearts. We wanted to write a guide for the gaslit women and girls (AFAB, AMAB, *all* of you) to say *yes*, this is happening to you. You are not alone. You do not have to fight this battle by yourself; we want to help you. Here's what happened to us, and here is how we got through it. Here are resources, facts, and statistics to arm yourself with so that you can take on the world with confidence as well as a realistic mindset, because you genuinely do need both to survive. We don't want you to feel as alone as we have over the last few decades. We don't want you to blame yourself for the shitty behavior you absorbed that made you doubt your worth, change your plans, abandon your dreams. We did that and ended up wasting years of our lives before we got to realize our dream of writing this book, which we hope will help you achieve every ambition you hold in your heart. We believe in you, and we believe we will see a significant change in our lifetime.

And just for the record, because we get this thrown at us quite often, we don't want, or need, a matriarchy. We don't need women to be in complete control of the world—that won't create the change we so desperately need. What we need is a breakdown of the power structures we've all been raised to believe in and trust. They benefit very few people, and in the end, the world has been—and continues to be—universally damaged because of them. We don't want anyone to walk away from this book thinking that the systems of control we've discussed are about individuals. Men are not the problem; the Patriarchy is—just as racism (and White supremacy) are the problems, not White people. Yes, we hold people accountable for bad behavior, but we also recognize the conditioning that made them who they are. We truly believe that no one is a lost cause, and everyone has the ability to change; it just has to matter enough to them. One of the things we hope this book accomplishes is to make it clear to women that they are facing very real problems in the workplace; it's too easy to blame ourselves for our own perceived failures or lack of success. When the system is built for someone else and rigged against you, it can feel very personal, but going down that road of self-blame leads to a huge expenditure of emotional energy, mental load, and personal time, all of which is wasted. Again, what we're fighting is not personal; they are systems of control. Their pervasiveness and deep roots in our societies' foundations is all down to length of exposure. These issues have been around a long time, and it will take a long time to see real change, but we can all work today to turn the tide. Maybe we won't see the full effects of our actions within our lifetimes, but generations to come will undoubtedly benefit from them.

And isn't that one of the compelling drives of being a human? We plant trees whose shade we won't live long enough to enjoy, but still we plant them, in the hope that their shade and beauty will benefit someone who will pass by long after we've gone.

ENDNOTES

1 Casey Gerald, "Embrace Your Raw, Strange Magic," filmed December 2018, TED Salon Belonging video, 16:55, https://www.ted.com/talks/casey_gerald_embrace_your_raw_strange_magic?language=en.

2 Campaign Against Living Miserably, *CALM Annual Report 2020–2021* (London: Campaign Against Living Miserably, 2021), https://www.thecalmzone.net/images/documents/CALM-Annual-Report-2020-21.pdf.

3 Hannah Ritchie, Max Roser, and Esteban Ortiz-Spinosa, "Suicide by Gender," *Our World in Data* (2015), https://ourworldindata.org/suicide#suicide-by-gender

4 Peggy McIntosh, *White Privilege and Male Privilege: A Personal Account of Coming to See Correspondences Through Work in Women's Studies*, 1988, https://www.collegeart.org/pdf/diversity/white-privilege-and-male-privilege.pdf.

5 Barry Deutsch, "An Unabashed Imitation of an Article by Peggy McIntosh," *Expository Magazine*, 2001–2, accessed March 2018, http://www.coloursofresistance.org/729/the-male-privilege-checklistan-unabashed-imitation-of-an-article-by-peggy-mcintosh/.

6 ——.

7 Olivia Petter, "Being a Mother is Equivalent to 2.5 Full-Time Jobs, Survey Finds," *Independent* (March 2018), https://www.independent.co.uk/life-style/health-and-families/mother-equivalent-2-jobs-full-time-childcare-98-hours-work-mum-survey-a8258676.html.

8 Jessica Grose, "Why Dads Don't Take Parental Leave," *New York Times*, February 19, 2020, https://www.nytimes.com/2020/02/19/parenting/why-dads-dont-take-parental-leave.html.

9 Jon Taylor, "Less than a Third of Eligible Men Take Paternity Leave," Latest, EMW LLP, July 8, 2019, https://www.emwllp.com/latest/less-than-a-third-of-men-take-paternity-leave/.

10 D. Clark, "Number of People Employed in the UK Construction Industry from First Quarter 2016 to Second Quarter 2020, by Gender," Economy, Statista, posted September 23, 2020, https://www.statista.com/statistics/1023964/employment-in-the-uk-construction-industry-by-gender/.

11 Randstad, *Women in Construction: Building Pace Post-Brexit* (Lufton: Randstad, 2020), https://email.randstad.co.uk/download-women-in-construction.

12 Claire Cain Miller, Kevin Quealy, and Margot Sanger-Katz, "The Top Jobs Where Women Are Outnumbered by Men Named John," *New York Times*, April 24, 2018, https://www.nytimes.com/interactive/2018/04/24/upshot/women-and-men-named-john.html.

13 The Associated Press, "In politics, women seriously outnumbered by men; less than 7% make world leaders, only 24% make lawmakers, says UN," First Post, World, posted March 13, 2019, https://www.firstpost.com/world/in-politics-women-seriously-outnumbered-by-men-less-than-7-make-world-leaders-only-24-make-lawmakers-says-un-6248411.html..

14 Aleksandra Sandstrom, "Women Relatively Rare in Top Positions of Religious Leadership," Pew Research Center, posted March 2, 2016, https://www.pewresearch.org/fact-tank/2016/03/02/women-relatively-rare-in-top-positions-of-religious-leadership/.

15 There has never been a female American president or secretary-general of the United Nations.

16 Nisha Arekapudi, "Over 100 Countries Still Bar Women from Working in Specific Jobs," London School of Economics, posted May 9, 2018, https://blogs.lse.ac.uk/businessreview/2018/05/09/over-100-countries-still-bar-women-from-working-in-specific-jobs/.

17 "Russia Opens 350 Banned Professions to Women, Stripping Soviet-Era Restrictions," Moscow Times, August 16, 2019, https://www.themoscowtimes.com/2019/08/16/russia-opens-350-banned-professions-to-women-stripping-soviet-era-restrictions-a66903.

18 Bethany Hughes, "Why Were Women Written Out of History? An Interview with Bethany Hughes," History Uncovered (blog), English Heritage, posted February 29, 2016, https://blog.english-heritage.org.uk/women-written-history-interview-bethany-hughes/.

19 Miki Kashtan, "Why Patriarchy Is Not About Men," Psychology Today, August 4, 2017, https://www.psychologytoday.com/gb/blog/acquired-spontaneity/201708/why-patriarchy-is-not-about-men.

20 Alberto Alesina, Paola Giuliano, and Nathan Nunn, "On the Origins of Gender Roles: Women and the Plough," Quarterly Journal of Economics 128, no. 2 (May 2013): 469–530, https://doi.org/10.1093/qje/qjt005.

21 Gerda Lerner, The Creation of the Patriarchy (New York City: Oxford University Press, 1987).

22 ——.

23 ——.

24 Hughes, "Women Written Out."

25 Lerner, The Creation.

26 Sharna Olfman, "Gender, Patriarchy, and Women's Mental Health: Psychoanalytic Perspectives," Journal of the American Academy of Psychoanalysis 22, no. 2 (June 1994): 259–71, https://doi.org/10.1521/jaap.1.1994.22.2.259.

27 Sigmund Freud, Three Essays on the Theory of Sexuality: The 1905 Edition (Brooklyn: Verso, 2017).

28 Eleanor Sawbridge Burton, "Sigmund Freud," Our Authors and Theorists, Institute of Psychoanalysis, posted 2015, https://psychoanalysis.org.uk/our-authors-and-theorists/sigmund-freud.

29 Olfman, "Women's Mental Health."

30 Caroline Criado-Perez, Invisible Women: Exposing Data Bias in a World Designed for Men (New York: Abrams Press, 2019).

31 Sarah Macharia and Marcus Burke, "Just 24% of News Sources Are Women. Here's Why That's a Problem," World Economic Forum, posted March 2, 2020, https://www.weforum.org/agenda/2020/03/women-representation-in-media/.

32 ——.
33 "Share of video game protagonists from 2015 to 2020, by gender," Statista, posted October 2020, https://www.statista.com/statistics/871912/character-gender-share-video-games/.
34 Criado-Perez, *Invisible Women.*
35 John Detrixhe, "US Women Will Take Control of an Additional $20 Trillion in Wealth This Decade," Quartz, July 29, 2020, https://qz.com/1885841/us-women-will-take-control-of-an-extra-19-trillion-in-wealth/.
36 Campaign Against Living Miserably, "CALM Impact."
37 Ritchie, Roser, and Ortiz-Spinosa, "Suicide."
38 Becky Frankiewicz, "5 Ways We Lack Gender Balance in the Workplace," Davos 2020, World Economic Forum, posted January 30, 2020, https://www.weforum.org/agenda/2020/01/5-ways-companies-can-progress-more-women-into-leadership-roles/.
39 Margaret M. Quinn and Peter M. Smith, "Gender, Work, and Health," *Annals of Work Exposures and Health* 62, no. 4 (May 2018): 389–92, https://doi.org/10.1093/annweh/wxy019.
40 Project Implicit, "Preliminary Information," Implicit Association Test, posted 2011, https://implicit.harvard.edu/implicit/takeatest.html.
41 Olfman, "Women's Mental Health."
42 "A Map of Gender-Diverse Cultures," PBS, posted August 11, 2015, https://www.pbs.org/independentlens/content/two-spirits_map-html/.
43 Alok Vaid-Menon, *Beyond the Gender Binary* (New York: Penguin Workshop, 2020).
44 Cade Hildreth, "Gender Spectrum: A Scientist Explains Why Gender Isn't Binary," *Blog, Cade Hildreth*, February 5, 2022, https://cadehildreth.com/gender-spectrum/.
45 "Education is the Premise of Progress," *Rwanda's Leading Daily, New Times,* December 6, 2010, https://www.newtimes.co.rw/section/read/96185.
46 Evelyn Brooks Higginbotham, *Righteous Discontent: The Women's Movement in the Black Baptist Church, 1880–1920* (Cambridge: Harvard University Press, 1993).
47 Minda Harts, *The Memo: What Women of Color Need to Know to Secure a Seat at the Table* (New York City: Seal Press, 2019).
48 ——.
49 "New CSI Research Reveals High Levels of Job Discrimination Faced by Ethnic Minorities in Britain," Centre for Social Investigation, posted January 18, 2019, http://csi.nuff.ox.ac.uk/?p=1299.
50 Sonia K. Kang et al., "Whitened Résumés: Race and Self-Presentation in the Labor Market," *Administrative Science Quarterly* 61, no. 3 March 2016): 469–502, https://doi.org/10.1177/0001839216639577.
51 Ella L. J. Edmondson Smith and Stella M. Nkomo, Our Separate Ways: *Black and White Women and the Struggle for Professional Identity* (Boston: Harvard Business School Press, 2001).
52 ——.
53 Zuhaira Washington and Laura M. Roberts, "Women of Color Get Less Support at Work. Here's How Managers Can Change That," *Harvard Business Review*, March 4, 2019, https://hbr.org/2019/03/women-of-color-get-less-support-at-work-heres-how-managers-can-change-that.
54 Smith and Nkomo, *Separate Ways.*
55 "Breadwinner Mothers by Race/Ethnicity," Quick Figures, Institute for Women's Policy Research, published April 2020, https://iwpr.org/wp-content/uploads/2020/05/QF-Breadwinner-Mothers-by-Race-FINAL-46.pdf.

56 Becky O'Connor, "Rise of the female breadwinner: Woman earns the most in one-in-four households," Royal London, posted May 27, 2020, https://www.royallondon.com/media/press-releases/archive/female-breadwinner-rise/.

57 "One Third of Mothers in Working Families Are Breadwinners in Britain," Press Releases, Institute for Public Policy, posted October 20, 2015, https://www.ippr.org/news-and-media/press-releases/one-third-of-mothers-in-working-families-are-breadwinners-in-britain.

58 "Healing a Divided Britain: The Need for a Comprehensive Race Equality Strategy," Publications Library, Equality and Human Rights Commission, posted August 18, 2016, https://www.equalityhumanrights.com/en/publication-download/healing-divided-britain-need-comprehensive-race-equality-strategy.

59 Hannah Westwater, Ella Glover, and Isabella McRae, "UK poverty: the facts, figures and effects," Social Justice, Big Issue, posted March 24, 2022, https://www.bigissue.com/news/social-justice/uk-poverty-the-facts-figures-and-effects/.

60 Bart Shaw et al., "Ethnicity, Gender and Social Mobility," Social Mobility Commission, published 2016, https://assets.publishing.service.gov.uk/government/uploads/system/uploads/attachment_data/file/579988/Ethnicity_gender_and_social_mobility.pdf.

61 "2021 Equal Pay Days," *Equal Pay Today*, http://www.equalpaytoday.org/overview-2021.

62 Tom Evans, "Ethnicity Pay Gaps in Great Britain: 2018," Earnings and Working Hours, Office for National Statistics, posted July 9, 2019, https://www.ons.gov.uk/employmentandlabourmarket/peopleinwork/earningsandworkinghours/articles/ethnicitypaygapsingreatbritain/2018.

63 Institute for Women's Policy Research, "Breadwinner Mothers."

64 McIntosh, *White Privilege*.

65 ——.

66 ——.

67 "Foreword: Jane Elliott – Shades of Noir: Journals," Shades of Noir, posted 2021, https://shadesofnoir.org.uk/journals/content/foreword-jane-elliott.

68 Harts, *The Memo*.

69 ——.

70 Stuart R. Levine and Thought Leaders, "Diversity Confirmed To Boost Innovation And Financial Results," *Forbes*, posted January 15, 2020, https://www.forbes.com/sites/forbesinsights/2020/01/15/diversity-confirmed-to-boost-innovation-and-financial-results/?sh=1a9abdc4a6a5.

71 James Baldwin, "A Report from Occupied Territory," *Nation*, July 11, 1966, https://www.thenation.com/article/culture/report-occupied-territory/.

72 Criado-Perez, *Invisible Women*.

73 "Women Shoulder the Responsibility of 'Unpaid Work,'" Earnings and Working Hours, Office for National Statistics, posted November 10, 2016, https://www.ons.gov.uk/employmentandlabourmarket/peopleinwork/earningsandworkinghours/articles/womenshouldertheresponsibilityofunpaidwork/2016-11-10.

74 Criado-Perez, *Invisible Women*.

75 "Work-Related Stress, Anxiety or Depression Statistics in Great Britain, 2021," Health and Safety Executive, published 2021, https://www.hse.gov.uk/statistics/causdis/stress.pdf.

76 Criado-Perez, *Invisible Women*.

77 "Women in the Workforce: Japan (Quick Take)," Research, Catalyst, posted November 24, 2020, https://www.catalyst.org/research/women-in-the-workforce-japan/.

78 Erin Reid, "Embracing, Passing, Revealing, and the Ideal Worker Image: How People Navigate Expected and Experienced Professional Identities," *Organization Science* 26, no. 4 (July–August 2015): 941–1261, https://doi.org/10.1287/orsc.2015.0975.

79 Criado-Perez, *Invisible Women*.

80 Christopher S. Payne, "Leisure Time in the UK," Satellite Accounts, Office for National Statistics, posted October 24, 2017, https://www.ons.gov.uk/economy/nationalaccounts/satelliteaccounts/articles/leisuretimeintheuk/2015.

81 Fanny Kilpi et al., "Living Arrangements as Determinants of Myocardial Infarction Incidence and Survival: A Prospective Register Study of Over 300,000 Finnish Men and Women," *Social Science and Medicine* 133, (May 2015): 93–100, https://doi.org/10.1016/j.socscimed.2015.03.054.

82 Grose, "Parental Leave."

83 Simon Usborne, "'It Was Seen as Weird': Why Are So Few Men Taking Shared Parental Leave?" *Guardian*, October 5, 2019, https://www.theguardian.com/lifeandstyle/2019/oct/05/shared-parental-leave-seen-as-weird-paternity-leave-in-decline.

84 Eliana Dockterman, "Gay Dads' Brains Develop Just Like Those of Straight Parents, Study Finds," *Time*, May 26, 2014, https://time.com/116843/gay-dads-brains-develop-just-like-those-of-straight-parents-study-finds/.

85 Branwen Jeffreys, "Do Children in Two-Parent Families Do Better?" BBC, February 5, 2019, https://www.bbc.co.uk/news/education-47057787.

86 Shelley J. Correll and Caroline Simard, "Research: Vague Feedback Is Holding Women Back," *Harvard Business Review*, April 29, 2016, https://hbr.org/2016/04/research-vague-feedback-is-holding-women-back.

87 D. Scott Lind et al., "Competency-Based Student Self-Assessment on a Surgery Rotation," *Journal of Surgical Research* 105, no. 1 (June 2002): 31–44, https://doi.org/10.1006/jsre.2002.6442.

88 Janie Boschma, "Why Women Don't Run for Office," Women Rule, Politico, June 12, 2017, https://www.politico.com/interactives/2017/women-rule-politics-graphic/.

89 Christina L. Exley and Judd B. Kessler, "The Gender Gap in Self-Promotion," National Bureau of Economic Research, published October 2019, revised May 2021, https://www.doi.org/10.3386/w26345.

90 Tara Sophia Mohr, "Why Women Don't Apply for Jobs Unless They're 100% Qualified," *Harvard Business Review*, August 25, 2014, https://hbr.org/2014/08/why-women-dont-apply-for-jobs-unless-theyre-100-qualified.

91 Joanne Lipman, "Women Are Still Not Asking for Pay Rises. Here's Why," Book Club, World Economic Forum, posted April 12, 2018, https://www.weforum.org/agenda/2018/04/women-are-still-not-asking-for-pay-rises-here-s-why/.

92 Louann Brizendine, *The Female Brain* (New York City: Broadway Books, 2006).

93 Anika Stuppy, "Why Power And Testosterone Are A Seriously Dangerous Mix," *Forbes*, posted July 25, 2018, https://www.forbes.com/sites/rsmdiscovery/2018/07/25/why-power-and-testosterone-are-a-seriously-dangerous-mix/?sh=7108ca595d98.

94 Wellcome Trust, "Testosterone Makes Us Less Cooperative and More Egocentric," Science News, Science Daily, posted January 31, 2012, www.sciencedaily.com/releases/2012/01/120131210259.htm.

95 Katty Kay and Claire Shipman, "The Confidence Gap," *Atlantic*, May 2014, https://www.theatlantic.com/magazine/archive/2014/05/the-confidence-gap/359815/.

96 ——.

97 ——.

98 Criado-Perez, *Invisible Women*.

99   Attracta Mooney, "Female Hedge Funds Outperform Those Run by Men," *Financial Times*, September 16, 2017, https://www.ft.com/content/8bffa2c4-99f3-11e7-a652-cde3f882dd7b.

100 Rocío Lorenzo et al., "How Diverse Leadership Teams Boost Innovation," Boston Consulting Group, posted January 23, 2018, https://www.bcg.com/publications/2018/how-diverse-leadership-teams-boost-innovation.

101 Jonathan Woetzel et al., "The Power of Parity: How Advancing Women's Equality Can Add $12 Trillion to Global Growth," McKinsey & Company, September 2015, https://www.mckinsey.com/~/media/mckinsey/industries/public%20and%20social%20sector/our%20insights/how%20advancing%20womens%20equality%20can%20add%2012%20trillion%20to%20global%20growth/mgi%20power%20of%20parity_full%20report_september%202015.pdf.

102 Riana Duncan, *That's an excellent suggestion, Miss Triggs. Perhaps one of the men here would like to make it*, 1988, cartoon showing a sexist boardroom, Modern Punch Cartoons, London, https://punch.photoshelter.com/image/I0000BaPhg4sVCD4.

103 Sean R. Martin, "Research: Men Get Credit for Voicing Ideas, but Not Problems. Women Don't Get Credit for Either," *Harvard Business Review*, November 2, 2017, https://hbr.org/2017/11/research-men-get-credit-for-voicing-ideas-but-not-problems-women-dont-get-credit-for-either.

104 Olivia Petter, "What is Hepeating?" *Independent*, November 29, 2017, https://www.independent.co.uk/life-style/hepeating-what-woman-ignore-men-idea-repeat-sexism-misogynist-a8080601.html.

105 Zameena Majia, "How to Combat 'Hepeating' at Work, According to a Harvard Professor," CNBC, updated October 11, 2017, https://www.cnbc.com/2017/10/11/how-to-combat-hepeating-at-work-according-to-a-harvard-professor.html.

106 ——.

107 Juliet Eilperin, "White House Women Want to be in the Room Where It Happens," *Washington Post*, September 13, 2016, https://www.washingtonpost.com/news/powerpost/wp/2016/09/13/white-house-women-are-now-in-the-room-where-it-happens/.

108 "Sisterhood," Cambridge Dictionary, accessed 2021, https://dictionary.cambridge.org/dictionary/english/sisterhood.

109 Radhika Sanghani, "Sisterhood Ceiling: Are Women Holding Each Other Back in the Workplace?" *Telegraph*, April 15, 2016, https://www.telegraph.co.uk/women/work/sisterhood-ceiling-are-women-really-holding-each-other-back-in-t/.

110 ——.

111 Sun Y. Lee, Selin Kesebir, and Madan M. Pillutla, "Gender Differences in Response to Competition with Same-Gender Coworkers: A Relational Perspective," *Journal of Personality and Social Psychology* 110, no. 6 (2016): 869–86, https://doi.org/10.1037/pspi0000051.

112 "Mind Survey Finds Men More Likely to Experience Work-Related Mental Health Problems," News, Mind, posted August 9, 2017, https://www.mind.org.uk/news-campaigns/news/mind-survey-finds-men-more-likely-to-experience-work-related-mental-health-problems/#.WZ6eBz596M.

113 "Key Data: Mental Health," Pro, Men's Health Forum, updated September 2017, https://www.menshealthforum.org.uk/key-data-mental-health.

114 Marguerite Rigoglioso, "Researchers: How Women Can Succeed in the Workplace," Management, Stanford Graduate School of Business, posted March 1, 2011, https://www.gsb.stanford.edu/insights/researchers-how-women-can-succeed-workplace.

115 Francesca Di Meglio, "Promotion Know-How for Women," Getting Promoted, Monster, https://www.monster.com/career-advice/article/promotion-know-how-for-women.

116 Kerry Hannon, "The No.1 Way Women Can Succeed at Work," *Forbes*, April 24, 2014, https://www.forbes.com/sites/nextavenue/2014/04/24/the-no-1-way-women-can-succeed-more-at-work/?sh=3db0db49b17c.

117 Daniel Bates, "Women Who Want to Succeed at Work Should Shut Up–While Men Who Want the Same Should Keep Talking, Research Says," *Daily Mail*, updated May 18, 2012, 10:30 a.m. EDT, https://www.dailymail.co.uk/news/article-2146015/Women-want-succeed-work-shut-men-want-talking.html.

118 Jane Mathews, "Katie Hopkins Says Women Should Sleep with Their Bosses to Get Ahead," *Daily Express*, July 24, 2014, 10:31 a.m., https://www.express.co.uk/news/uk/491280/Katie-Hopkins-says-women-should-sleep-with-their-bosses-to-get-ahead.

119 Ruchika Tulshyan, "Women and Office Politics: Play the Game or Lose," *Forbes*, November 20, 2013, https://www.forbes.com/sites/ruchikatulshyan/2013/11/20/women-and-office-politics-play-the-game-or-lose/?sh=14c145dfa8d2.

120 Lisa Unwin and Deborah Khan, "Women, Play the Long Game," Organizations and People, Strategy + Business, posted February 2, 2017, https://www.strategy-business.com/blog/Women-Play-the-Long-Game.

121 "Humble," Cambridge Dictionary, accessed 2021, https://dictionary.cambridge.org/dictionary/english/humble.

122 Amy Poehler, *Yes Please* (New York: HarperCollins, 2014).

123 Randstad, *Post-Brexit*.

124 Robby Berman, "Women Are More Productive Than Men, According to New Research," Education, Skills, and Learning, World Economic Forum, posted October 8, 2018, https://www.weforum.org/agenda/2018/10/women-are-more-productive-than-men-at-work-these-days.

125 Petter, "Being a Mother."

126 Linda Dierks, "5 Tips to Cultivate Personal Power and Self-Confidence," Personal Growth, Chopra, posted July 20, 2018, https://www.chopra.com/articles/5-tips-to-cultivate-personal-power-and-self-confidence.

127 GOOP Podcast, "Gwyneth x Oprah: Power, Perception & Soul Purpose," March 8, 2018, produced by Gwyneth Paltrow along with Boll & Branch, podcast, 1:16:01, https://goop.com/the-goop-podcast/gwyneth-x-oprah-power-perception-soul-purpose/.

128 Tammy D. Allen, Mark L. Poteet, and Susan M. Burroughs, "The Mentor's Perspective: A Qualitative Inquiry and Future Research Agenda," *Journal of Vocational Behavior* 51, no. 1 (August 1997): 70–89, https://doi.org/10.1006/jvbe.1997.1596.

129 Kate Ashford, "Are Men Afraid To Mentor Women?" LearnVest, *Forbes*, May 3, 2013, https://www.forbes.com/sites/learnvest/2013/05/03/are-men-afraid-to-mentor-women/?sh=1ef4dac62481.

130 Michelle Fox, "The 'Motherhood Penalty' Is Real, and It Costs Women $16,000 a Year in Lost Wages," Closing the Gap, CNBC, updated March 25, 2019, https://www.cnbc.com/2019/03/25/the-motherhood-penalty-costs-women-16000-a-year-in-lost-wages.html.

131 Charles Hymas, "Women Face 'Motherhood Penalty' of Up to 45 Percent Lower Earnings," *Telegraph*, July 27, 2019, 9:00 p.m. GMT, https://www.telegraph.co.uk/news/2021/07/27/women-face-motherhood-penalty-45-per-cent-lower-earnings/.

132 Fox, "$16,000 a Year."

133 Sean Coughlan, "'Motherhood Penalty' in Worse Pay at Work," Education, BBC, posted April 11, 2017, https://www.bbc.co.uk/news/education-39566746.

134 Giselle Cory and Alfie Stirling, "Pay and Parenthood: An Analysis of Wage Inequality Between Mums and Dads," TouchStone Extra, Trade Unions Congress, 2016, https://www.tuc.org.uk/sites/default/files/Pay_and_Parenthood_Touchstone_Extra_2016_LR.pdf.

135 Damian Grimshaw and Jill Rubery, "The Motherhood Pay Gap: A Review of the Issues, Theory, and International Evidence," European Institute for Gender Equality, International Labour Office, https://eige.europa.eu/resources/wcms_371804.pdf.

136 ——.

137 Marissa Orr, *Lean Out: The Truth about Women, Power, and the Workplace* (Nashville: HarperCollins Leadership, 2019).

138 Estelle Erasmus, "Why Author Marissa Orr Leaned Out Instead of In, and How You Can Too," *Forbes*, May 26, 2019, https://www.forbes.com/sites/estelleerasmus/2019/05/26/why-author-marissa-orr-leaned-out-instead-of-in-and-how-you-can-too/?sh=bd04422e80e2.

139 Darla Mercado, "Here's the Ken Fisher Audio that Inflamed Executives at a Financial Conference," Personal Finance, CNBC, posted October 11, 2019.

140 Beverly Engel, "How Being Too Nice Can Be Dangerous for Women," *Psychology Today*, August 8, 2019, https://www.psychologytoday.com/us/blog/the-compassion-chronicles/201908/how-being-too-nice-can-be-dangerous-women.

141 ——.

142 Suzannah Weiss, "Women's Value Doesn't Just Lie in Pleasing Others," *Bustle*, August 15, 2016, https://www.bustle.com/articles/178718-6-ways-women-are-taught-to-please-other-people-why-they-dont-have-to.

143 Deborah Lupton, "What Does Fat Discrimination Look Like?" *Conversation*, January 2, 2013, https://theconversation.com/what-does-fat-discrimination-look-like-10247.

144 Ruth Lewis and Cicely Marston, "Oral Sex, Young People, and Gendered Narratives of Reciprocity," *Journal of Sex Research* 53, no. 7 (September 2016): 776–87, https://doi.org/10.1080/00224499.2015.1117564.

145 Julie Bindel, "The Truth About the Porn Industry," *Guardian*, July 2, 2010, https://www.theguardian.com/lifeandstyle/2010/jul/02/gail-dines-pornography.

146 ——.

147 Chimamanda N. Adichie, *We Should All Be Feminists* (London: Fourth Estate, 2014).

148 *Saturday Night Live*, season 33, episode 5, "Weekend Update," directed by Don Roy King, written by Seth Meyers, Paula Pell, and Andrew Steele, featuring Tina Fey, Carrie Underwood, Amber Lee Ettinger, Steve Martin, Mike Huckabee, Don Pardo, and Casey Wilson, aired February 23, 2008, on NBC, https://www.nbc.com/saturday-night-live/video/february-23-tina-fey/4017406.

149 "What Is Street Harassment?" About, Stop Street Harassment, updated March 2015, https://stopstreetharassment.org/about/what-is-street-harassment/.

150 UC San Diego Center on Gender Equity and Health, "Measuring #Me Too: A National Study on Sexual Harassment and Assault," Stop Street Harassment, April 2019, https://stopstreetharassment.org/wp-content/uploads/2012/08/2019-MeToo-National-Sexual-Harassment-and-Assault-Report.pdf.

151 ——.

152 "Survey: Street Harassment and Age," National Studies, Stop Street Harassment, 2019, https://stopstreetharassment.org/our-work/nationalstudy/shage/.

153 Renata Buongiorno et al., "Why Women Are Blamed for Being Sexually Harassed: The Effects of Empathy for Female Victims and Male Perpetrators," *Psychology of Women Quarterly* 44, no. 1 (August 2019): 11–27, https://doi.org/10.1177/0361684319868730.
154 "Still Just a Bit of Banter? Sexual Harassment in the Workplace in 2016," Trade Union Congress, 2016, https://www.tuc.org.uk/sites/default/files/SexualHarassmentreport2016.pdf.
155 Kim Parker, "Women in Majority-Male Workplaces Report Higher Rates of Gender Discrimination," Gender Equality and Discrimination, Pew Research Center, posted March 7, 2018, https://www.pewresearch.org/fact-tank/2018/03/07/women-in-majority-male-workplaces-report-higher-rates-of-gender-discrimination/.
156 "Sexual Harassment of Disabled Women in the Workplace," Research and Analysis, Trade Union Congress, posted July 19, 2021, https://www.tuc.org.uk/research-analysis/reports/sexual-harassment-disabled-women-workplace.
157 "End Sexual Harassment in the Workplace," News Listing, Trade Union Congress, posted January 17, 2020, https://www.tuc.org.uk/news/end-sexual-harassment-workplace.
158 Trade Union Congress, "Bit of Banter?"
159 ——.
160 ——, "Disabled Women."
161 ——, "Bit of Banter?"
162 ——.
163 "Women's Mental Health Issues—Not to Be Ignored at Work," Unison the Public Service Union, February 2017, https://www.unison.org.uk/content/uploads/2017/02/24227.pdf.
164 Meghan Rabbitt, "How to Address Mental Health In the Workplace," *Woman's Day*, January 21, 2020, https://www.womansday.com/life/a30501058/mental-health-in-the-workplace/.
165 "Human Connection in the Virtual Workplace," The HOW Institute for Society, March 2021, https://thehowinstitute.org/wp-content/uploads/2021/03/HOW_Institute_Human_Connection_Report_single-pages.pdf.
166 Liz Hilton Segel and Kana Enomoto, "5 Ways Employers Can Support Women's Mental Health," *Harvard Business Review,* June 11, 2021, https://hbr.org/2021/06/5-ways-employers-can-support-womens-mental-health.
167 Connor Holmes, "What Employers Can Do to Support Women's Mental Health," Mental Health, Spring Health, posted March 22, 2021, https://www.springhealth.com/what-employers-can-do-to-support-womens-mental-health/.
168 Hayley Smith, "'Just Living with Pain': Women's Healthcare Waylaid by COVID-19 Pandemic," *Los Angeles Times*, updated February 22, 2021, 7:29 a.m. PT, https://www.latimes.com/california/story/2021-02-22/covid-19-pandemic-womens-wellness-effects.
169 Amit Sud et al., "Effect of Delays in the 2-Week-Wait Cancer Referral Pathway During the COVID-19 Pandemic on Cancer Survival in the UK: A Modelling Study," *Lancet Oncology* 21, no. 8 (August 2020): 1035–44, https://doi.org/10.1016/S1470-2045(20)30392-2.
170 Garen Staglin, "Employers Must Rise to the Challenge of Supporting Women in the Workplace," *Forbes*, M0, 2021, https://www.forbes.com/sites/onemind/2021/03/10/employers-must-rise-to-the-challenge-of-supporting-women-in-the-workplace/?sh=2c5e56f11496.

171 Kimberly Querry, "Oklahoma City Apartment Complex Catches Fire, 5 Units Damaged; Sweet Brown Explains," Oklahoma News 4: KFOR-TV, updated April 9, 2012, 11:13 a.m. CDT, https://kfor.com/news/okc-apartment-complex-catches-fire-5-units-damaged/.

172 S. E. Taylor et al., "Biobehavioral Responses to Stress in Females: Tend-and-Befriend, Not Fight-or-Flight," *Psychological Review* 107, no. 3 (July 2000): 411–29, https://doi.org/10.1037/0033-295x.107.3.411.

173 Anupriya Narsaria, "Why Are Boys Not Allowed to Play with Dolls?" Science ABC, updated January 22, 2022, https://www.scienceabc.com/social-science/why-are-boys-not-allowed-to-play-with-dolls.html.

174 American Addiction Centers National Rehabs Directory, "An Epidemic of Body Hatred," Explore, Dying to be Barbie | Eating Disorders in Pursuit of the Impossible, posted 2013, https://rehabs.com/explore/dying-to-be-barbie/.

175 Jennifer Sky, "Does Fashion Week Exploit Teen Models?" *Daily Beast*, July 12, 2017, 6:27p.m. ET, https://www.thedailybeast.com/does-fashion-week-exploit-teen-models.

176 Maya Singer, "Why the Fashion World Needs to Commit to an 18+ Modeling Standard," *Vogue*, August 16, 2018, https://www.vogue.com/article/why-fashion-needs-to-commit-to-age-appropiate-modeling-standard-vogue-september-2018.

177 American Addiction Centers National Rehabs Directory, "Body Hatred."

178 Claire Bates, "How Does 'Curvy Barbie' Compare with an Average Woman?" *BBC News*, March 3, 2016, https://www.bbc.co.uk/news/magazine-35670446.

179 Canadian Broadcasting Company, "Instagram Fuels Both Body-image Issues and Social Connections, Teen Girls Say," Yahoo! News, posted October 6, 2021, https://ca.news.yahoo.com/instagram-fuels-both-body-image-080000249.html.

180 Deborah A. Christel and Susan C. Dunn, "Average American Women's Clothing Size: Comparing National Health and Nutritional Examination Surveys (1988–2010) to ASTM International Misses and Women's Plus Size Clothing," *International Journal of Fashion Design, Technology and Education* 10, no. 2 (August 2016): 129–36, https://doi.org/10.1080/17543266.2016.1214291.

181 Fashion United, "Redefining Plus Size – Dressing the 'Average' Woman in Europe," News, Business, posted January 14, 2020, https://fashionunited.uk/news/business/redefining-plus-size-dressing-the-average-woman-in-europe/2020011447030.

182 Brid Costello, "Kate Moss: The Waif That Roared," Beauty Features, Women's Wear Daily, posted November 13, 2009, https://wwd.com/beauty-industry-news/beauty-features/kate-moss-the-waif-that-roared-2367932/.

183 Naomi Wolf, *The Beauty Myth* (London: Chatto & Windus, 1990).

184 Gianluca Russo, "How Fatphobia Has Cemented Itself in the American Workplace," Beauty, Nylon, posted November 30, 2020, https://www.nylon.com/beauty/how-fatphobia-has-cemented-itself-in-the-american-workplace.

185 Tessa E. Charlesworth and Mahzarin R. Banaji, "Patterns of Implicit and Explicit Attitudes: I. Long-Term Change and Stability From 2007 to 2016," *Association for Psychological Science* 30, no. 2 (February 2019): 174–92, https://doi.org/10.1177/0956797618813087.

186 W. F. Ferris and N. J. Crowther, "Once Fat Was Fat and That Was That: Our Changing Perspectives on Adipose Tissue," *Cardiovascular Journal of Africa* 22, no. 3 (June 2011): 147–54, https://doi.org/10.5830/cvja-2010-083.

187 Aubrey Gordon, "'Fat' Isn't a Bad Word—It's Just the Way I Describe My Body," Opinion, Self, posted May 28, 2021, https://www.self.com/story/fat-isnt-bad-word.

188 Rebecca Puhl and Kelly D. Brownell, "Bias, Discrimination, and Obesity," *Wiley Obesity Reviews* 12, no. 9 (September 2012): 788–805, https://doi.org/10.1038/oby.2001.108.

189 Amanda Gardner, "Many Obese Americans Struggle With Stigma, Discrimination, Poll Finds," Health Day, posted August 23, 2012, https://consumer.healthday.com/vitamins-and-nutrition-information-27/obesity-health-news-505/many-obese-americans-struggle-with-stigma-discrimination-poll-finds-667697.html.

190 Zofia Bajorek and Stephen Bevan, "Obesity Stigma at Work: Improving Inclusion and Productivity," Institute for Employment Studies, posted 2020, https://www.employment-studies.co.uk/system/files/resources/files/Obesity%20Stigma%20at%20Work%20-%20Improving%20Inclusion%20and%20Productivity_0.pdf.

191 Jennifer Bennett Shinall, "Occupational Characteristics and the Obesity Wage Penalty," SSRN, revised April 30, 2016, https://papers.ssrn.com/sol3/papers.cfm?abstract_id=2379575.

192 Angelina R. Sutin, Yannick Stephan, and Antonio Terracciano, "Weight Discrimination and Risk of Mortality," *Psychological Science* 26, no. 11 (September 2015): 1803–11, https://doi.org/10.1177/0956797615601103.

193 Zofia and Bevan, "Obesity Stigma."

194 "Women in the Workplace: Women with Disabilities," Lean In and McKinsey & Company, posted September 2021, https://leanin.org/article/women-in-the-workplace-women-with-disabilities.

195 "Advancing Women and Girls with Disabilities," USAID, posted May 7, 2019, https://www.usaid.gov/what-we-do/gender-equality-and-womens-empowerment/women-disabilities.

196 Trade Union Congress, "Disabled Women."

197 Robyn Powell, "How to Include Disabled Women in the Fight for Equal Pay," News, Bustle, posted April 10, 2018, https://www.bustle.com/p/disabled-womens-equal-pay-struggles-often-go-unheard-but-you-can-help-include-them-8730123

198 USAID, "Advancing Women."

199 Powell, "Equal Pay."

200 Lean In and McKinsey & Company, "Women in the Workplace."

201 ——.

202 Trade Union Congress, "Disabled Women."

203 ——.

204 USAID, "Advancing Women."

205 American Psychological Association, "Working Out Boosts Brain Health," Psychology Topics, Exercise Fitness, posted March 4, 2020, https://www.apa.org/topics/exercise-fitness/stress.

206 Maggie Germano, "Women are Working More Than Ever, but They Still Take on Most Household Responsibilities," *Forbes*, posted March 27, 2019, https://www.forbes.com/sites/maggiegermano/2019/03/27/women-are-working-more-than-ever-but-they-still-take-on-most-household-responsibilities/?sh=46a83bb752e9.

207 "Women and Financial Wellness: Beyond the Bottom Line," Merrill Lynch (blog), https://agewave.com/what-we-do/landmark-research-and-consulting/research-studies/women-and-financial-wellness/.

208 Bryan Borzykowski, "Successful Executives and the Four-hour Sleep Myth," Worklife, BBC, posted November 3, 2014, https://www.bbc.com/worklife/article/20130726-the-sleep-secrets-of-ceos.

209 Harvey R. Colten and Bruce M. Altevogt, eds., *Sleep Disorders and Sleep Deprivation: An Unmet Public Health Problem* (Washington: National Academies Press, 2006).

210 Amanda Holpuch, "The 'Shecession': Why Economic Crisis is affecting Women More Than Men," *Guardian*, August 4, 2020, Economics, https://www.theguardian.com/business/2020/aug/04/shecession-coronavirus-pandemic-economic-fallout-women.

211 "COVID-19 Cost Women Globally Over $800 Billion in Lost Income in One Year," Press Releases, Oxfam International, posted April 29, 2021, https://www.oxfam.org/en/press-releases/covid-19-cost-women-globally-over-800-billion-lost-income-one-year.

212 Deloitte, *Women @ Work: A Global Outlook* (London: Deloitte, 2022), https://www2.deloitte.com/content/dam/Deloitte/global/Documents/deloitte-women-at-work-2022-a-global-outlook.pdf.

213 ——.

214 ——.

215 Lean In and McKinsey & Company, "Women in the Workplace."

216 "When Hard Work Is Not Enough: Women in Low-paid Jobs," National Women's Law Center, posted 2020, https://nwlc.org/wp-content/uploads/2020/04/Women-in-Low-Paid-Jobs-report_ES_pp01.pdf.

217 Lean In and McKinsey & Company, "Women in the Workplace."

218 Tirion Havard, "Domestic Abuse and Covid-19: A Year into the Pandemic," Insight, House of Commons Library, posted May 11, 2021, https://commonslibrary.parliament.uk/domestic-abuse-and-covid-19-a-year-into-the-pandemic/.

219 Brad Boserup, Mark McKenney, and Adele Elkbuli, "Alarming Trends in US Domestic Violence During the COVID-19 Pandemic," *American Journal of Emergency Medicine* 38, no. 12 (December 2020): 2753–5, https://doi.org/10.1016/j.ajem.2020.04.077.

220 "Keeping Girls in the Picture," UNESCO, posted 2020, https://en.unesco.org/covid19/educationresponse/girlseducation.

221 "Global Gender Gap Report 2021," World Economic Forum, posted March 2021, https://www3.weforum.org/docs/WEF_GGGR_2021.pdf.

BIBLIOGRAPHY

"2021 Equal Pay Days." *Equal Pay Today*. http://www.equalpaytoday.org/overview-2021.

"A Map of Gender-Diverse Cultures." PBS. Posted August 11, 2015. https://www.pbs.org/independentlens/content/two-spirits_map-html/.

"Advancing Women and Girls with Disabilities." USAID. Posted May 7, 2019. https://www.usaid.gov/what-we-do/gender-equality-and-womens-empowerment/women-disabilities.

"Breadwinner Mothers by Race/Ethnicity." Quick Figures. Institute for Women's Policy Research. Published April 2020. https://iwpr.org/wp-content/uploads/2020/05/QF-Breadwinner-Mothers-by-Race-FINAL-46.pdf.

"COVID-19 Cost Women Globally Over $800 Billion in Lost Income in One Year." Press Releases. Oxfam International. Posted April 29, 2021. https://www.oxfam.org/en/press-releases/covid-19-cost-women-globally-over-800-billion-lost-income-one-year.

"Education is the Premise of Progress." *Rwanda's Leading Daily*. New Times. December 6, 2010. https://www.newtimes.co.rw/section/read/96185.

"End Sexual Harassment in the Workplace." News Listing. Trade Union Congress. Posted January 17, 2020. https://www.tuc.org.uk/news/end-sexual-harassment-workplace.

"Foreword: Jane Elliott – Shades of Noir: Journals." Shades of Noir. Posted 2021. https://shadesofnoir.org.uk/journals/content/foreword-jane-elliott.

"Global Gender Gap Report 2021." World Economic Forum. Posted March 2021. https://www3.weforum.org/docs/WEF_GGGR_2021.pdf.

"Healing a Divided Britain: The Need for a Comprehensive Race Equality Strategy." Publications Library. Equality and Human Rights Commission. Posted August 18, 2016. https://www.equalityhumanrights.com/en/publication-download/healing-divided-britain-need-comprehensive-race-equality-strategy.

"Human Connection in the Virtual Workplace." The HOW Institute for Society. March 2021. https://thehowinstitute.org/wp-content/uploads/2021/03/HOW_Institute_ Human_Connection_Report_single-pages.pdf.

"Humble." Cambridge Dictionary. Accessed 2021. https://dictionary.cambridge.org/ dictionary/english/humble.

"Keeping Girls in the Picture." UNESCO. Posted 2020. https://en.unesco.org/covid19/ educationresponse/girlseducation.

"Key Data: Mental Health." Pro. Men's Health Forum. Updated September 2017. https:// www.menshealthforum.org.uk/key-data-mental-health.

"Mind Survey Finds Men More Likely to Experience Work-Related Mental Health Problems." News. Mind. Posted August 9, 2017. https://www.mind.org.uk/news- campaigns/news/mind-survey-finds-men-more-likely-to-experience-work-related- mental-health-problems/#.WZ6eBz596M.

"New CSI Research Reveals High Levels of Job Discrimination Faced by Ethnic Minorities in Britain." Centre for Social Investigation. Posted January 18, 2019. http://csi.nuff. ox.ac.uk/?p=1299.

"One Third of Mothers in Working Families Are Breadwinners in Britain." Press Releases. Institute for Public Policy. Posted October 20, 2015. https://www.ippr.org/news-and- media/press-releases/one-third-of-mothers-in-working-families-are-breadwinners-in- britain.

"Russia Opens 350 Banned Professions to Women, Stripping Soviet-Era Restrictions." Moscow Times. August 16, 2019. https://www.themoscowtimes.com/2019/08/16/russia- opens-350-banned-professions-to-women-stripping-soviet-era-restrictions-a66903.

"Sexual Harassment of Disabled Women in the Workplace." Research and Analysis. Trade Union Congress. Posted July 19, 2021. https://www.tuc.org.uk/research-analysis/ reports/sexual-harassment-disabled-women-workplace.

"Share of video game protagonists from 2015 to 2020, by gender." Statista. Posted October 2020. https://www.statista.com/statistics/871912/character-gender-share-video- games/.

"Sisterhood." Cambridge Dictionary. Accessed 2021. https://dictionary.cambridge.org/ dictionary/english/sisterhood.

"Still Just a Bit of Banter? Sexual Harassment in the Workplace in 2016." Trade Union Congress. 2016. https://www.tuc.org.uk/sites/default/files/SexualHarassmentreport2016. pdf.

"Survey: Street Harassment and Age." National Studies. Stop Street Harassment. 2019. https://stopstreetharassment.org/our-work/nationalstudy/shage/.

"What Is Street Harassment?" About. Stop Street Harassment. Updated March 2015. https://stopstreetharassment.org/about/what-is-street-harassment/.

"When Hard Work Is Not Enough: Women in Low-paid Jobs." National Women's Law Center. Posted 2020. https://nwlc.org/wp-content/uploads/2020/04/Women-in-Low-Paid-Jobs-report_ES_pp01.pdf.

"Women and Financial Wellness: Beyond the Bottom Line." Merrill Lynch (blog). https://agewave.com/what-we-do/landmark-research-and-consulting/research-studies/women-and-financial-wellness/.

"Women in the Workforce: Japan (Quick Take)." Research. Catalyst. Posted November 24, 2020. https://www.catalyst.org/research/women-in-the-workforce-japan/.

"Women in the Workplace: Women with Disabilities." Lean In and McKinsey & Company. Posted September 2021. https://leanin.org/article/women-in-the-workplace-women-with-disabilities.

"Women Shoulder the Responsibility of 'Unpaid Work.'" Earnings and Working Hours. Office for National Statistics. Posted November 10, 2016. https://www.ons.gov.uk/employmentandlabourmarket/peopleinwork/earningsandworkinghours/articles/womenshouldertheresponsibilityofunpaidwork/2016-11-10.

"Women's Mental Health Issues—Not to Be Ignored at Work." Unison the Public Service Union. February 2017. https://www.unison.org.uk/content/uploads/2017/02/24227.pdf.

"Work-Related Stress, Anxiety or Depression Statistics in Great Britain, 2021." Health and Safety Executive. Published 2021. https://www.hse.gov.uk/statistics/causdis/stress.pdf.

Adichie, Chimamanda N. *We Should All Be Feminists*. London: Fourth Estate, 2014.

Alesina, Alberto, Paola Giuliano, and Nathan Nunn. "On the Origins of Gender Roles: Women and the Plough." *Quarterly Journal of Economics* 128, no. 2 (May 2013): 469–530. https://doi.org/10.1093/qje/qjt005.

Allen, Tammy D., Mark L. Poteet, and Susan M. Burroughs. "The Mentor's Perspective: A Qualitative Inquiry and Future Research Agenda." *Journal of Vocational Behavior* 51, no. 1 (August 1997): 70–89. https://doi.org/10.1006/jvbe.1997.1596.

American Addiction Centers National Rehabs Directory. "An Epidemic of Body Hatred." Explore. Dying to be Barbie | Eating Disorders in Pursuit of the Impossible. Posted 2013. https://rehabs.com/explore/dying-to-be-barbie/.

American Psychological Association. "Working Out Boosts Brain Health." Psychology Topics. Exercise Fitness. Posted March 4, 2020. https://www.apa.org/topics/exercise-fitness/stress.

Arekapudi, Nisha. "Over 100 Countries Still Bar Women from Working in Specific Jobs." London School of Economics. Posted May 9, 2018. https://blogs.lse.ac.uk/businessreview/2018/05/09/over-100-countries-still-bar-women-from-working-in-specific-jobs/.

Ashford, Kate. "Are Men Afraid To Mentor Women?" LearnVest. *Forbes*. May 3, 2013. https://www.forbes.com/sites/learnvest/2013/05/03/are-men-afraid-to-mentor-women/?sh=1ef4dac62481.

Associated Press, The. "In politics, women seriously outnumbered by men; less than 7% make world leaders, only 24% make lawmakers, says UN." First Post. World. Posted March 13, 2019. https://www.firstpost.com/world/in-politics-women-seriously-outnumbered-by-men-less-than-7-make-world-leaders-only-24-make-lawmakers-says-un-6248411.html.

Bajorek, Zofia, and Stephen Bevan. "Obesity Stigma at Work: Improving Inclusion and Productivity." Institute for Employment Studies. Posted 2020. https://www.employment-studies.co.uk/system/files/resources/files/Obesity%20Stigma%20at%20Work%20-%20Improving%20Inclusion%20and%20Productivity_0.pdf.

Baldwin, James. "A Report from Occupied Territory." *Nation*. July 11, 1966. https://www.thenation.com/article/culture/report-occupied-territory/.

Bates, Claire. "How Does 'Curvy Barbie' Compare with an Average Woman?" *BBC News*. March 3, 2016. https://www.bbc.co.uk/news/magazine-35670446.

Bates, Daniel. "Women Who Want to Succeed at Work Should Shut Up–While Men Who Want the Same Should Keep Talking, Research Says." *Daily Mail*. Updated May 18, 2012, 10:30 a.m. EDT. https://www.dailymail.co.uk/news/article-2146015/Women-want-succeed-work-shut-men-want-talking.html.

Berman, Robby. "Women Are More Productive Than Men, According to New Research." Education, Skills, and Learning. World Economic Forum. Posted October 8, 2018. https://www.weforum.org/agenda/2018/10/women-are-more-productive-than-men-at-work-these-days.

Bindel, Julie. "The Truth About the Porn Industry." *Guardian*. July 2, 2010. https://www.theguardian.com/lifeandstyle/2010/jul/02/gail-dines-pornography.

Borzykowski, Bryan. "Successful Executives and the Four-hour Sleep Myth." Worklife. BBC. Posted November 3, 2014. https://www.bbc.com/worklife/article/20130726-the-sleep-secrets-of-ceos.

Boschma, Janie. "Why Women Don't Run for Office." Women Rule. Politico. June 12, 2017. https://www.politico.com/interactives/2017/women-rule-politics-graphic/.

Boserup, Brad, Mark McKenney, and Adele Elkbuli. "Alarming Trends in US Domestic Violence During the COVID-19 Pandemic." *American Journal of Emergency Medicine* 38, no. 12 (December 2020): 2753–5. https://doi.org/10.1016/j.ajem.2020.04.077.

Brizendine, Louann. *The Female Brain*. New York City: Broadway Books, 2006.

Buongiorno, Renata, Chloe Langbroek, Paul G. Bain, Michelle Ting, and Michelle K. Ryan. "Why Women Are Blamed for Being Sexually Harassed: The Effects of Empathy for Female Victims and Male Perpetrators." *Psychology of Women Quarterly* 44, no. 1 (August 2019): 11–27. https://doi.org/10.1177/0361684319868730.

Burton, Eleanor Sawbridge. "Sigmund Freud." Our Authors and Theorists. Institute of Psychoanalysis. Posted 2015. https://psychoanalysis.org.uk/our-authors-and-theorists/sigmund-freud.

Campaign Against Living Miserably. *CALM Impact Report 2019–2020*. London: Campaign Against Living Miserably, 2021. https://www.thecalmzone.net/images/documents/CALM-Annual-Report-2020-21.pdf.

Canadian Broadcasting Company. "Instagram Fuels Both Body-image Issues and Social Connections, Teen Girls Say." Yahoo! News. Posted October 6, 2021. https://ca.news.yahoo.com/instagram-fuels-both-body-image-080000249.html.

Charlesworth, Tessa E., and Mahzarin R. Banaji. "Patterns of Implicit and Explicit Attitudes: I. Long-Term Change and Stability From 2007 to 2016." *Association for Psychological Science* 30, no. 2 (February 2019): 174–92. https://doi.org/10.1177/0956797618813087.

Christel, Deborah A., and Susan C. Dunn. "Average American Women's Clothing Size: Comparing National Health and Nutritional Examination Surveys (1988–2010) to ASTM International Misses and Women's Plus Size Clothing." *International Journal of Fashion Design, Technology and Education* 10, no. 2 (August 2016): 129–36. https://doi.org/10.1080/17543266.2016.1214291.

Clark, D. "Number of People Employed in the UK Construction Industry from First Quarter 2016 to Second Quarter 2020, by Gender." Economy. Statista. Posted September 23, 2020. https://www.statista.com/statistics/1023964/employment-in-the-uk-construction-industry-by-gender/.

Colten, Harvey R., and Bruce M. Altevogt, eds. *Sleep Disorders and Sleep Deprivation: An Unmet Public Health Problem*. Washington: National Academies Press, 2006.

Correll, Shelley J., and Caroline Simard. "Research: Vague Feedback Is Holding Women Back." *Harvard Business Review*. April 29, 2016. https://hbr.org/2016/04/research-vague-feedback-is-holding-women-back.

Cory, Giselle, and Alfie Stirling. "Pay and Parenthood: An Analysis of Wage Inequality Between Mums and Dads." TouchStone Extra. Trade Unions Congress. Posted 2016. https://www.tuc.org.uk/sites/default/files/Pay_and_Parenthood_Touchstone_Extra_2016_LR.pdf.

Costello, Brid. "Kate Moss: The Waif That Roared." Beauty Features. Women's Wear Daily. Posted November 13, 2009. https://wwd.com/beauty-industry-news/beauty-features/kate-moss-the-waif-that-roared-2367932/.

Coughlan, Sean. "'Motherhood Penalty' in Worse Pay at Work." Education. BBC. Posted April 11, 2017. https://www.bbc.co.uk/news/education-39566746.

Criado-Perez, Caroline. *Invisible Women: Exposing Data Bias in a World Designed for Men*. New York: Abrams Press, 2019.

Deloitte. *Women @ Work: A Global Outlook*. London: Deloitte, 2022. https://www2.deloitte.com/content/dam/Deloitte/global/Documents/deloitte-women-at-work-2022-a-global-outlook.pdf.

Detrixhe, John. "US Women Will Take Control of an Additional $20 Trillion in Wealth This Decade." Quartz. July 29, 2020. https://qz.com/1885841/us-women-will-take-control-of-an-extra-19-trillion-in-wealth/.

Deutsch, Barry. "An Unabashed Imitation of an Article by Peggy McIntosh." *Expository Magazine*, 2001–2. Accessed March 2018. http://www.coloursofresistance.org/729/the-male-privilege-checklistan-unabashed-imitation-of-an-article-by-peggy-mcintosh/.

Di Meglio, Francesca. "Promotion Know-How for Women." Getting Promoted. Monster. https://www.monster.com/career-advice/article/promotion-know-how-for-women.

Dierks, Linda. "5 Tips to Cultivate Personal Power and Self-Confidence." Personal Growth. Chopra. Posted July 20, 2018. https://www.chopra.com/articles/5-tips-to-cultivate-personal-power-and-self-confidence.

Dockterman, Eliana. "Gay Dads' Brains Develop Just Like Those of Straight Parents, Study Finds." *Time*. May 26, 2014. https://time.com/116843/gay-dads-brains-develop-just-like-those-of-straight-parents-study-finds/.

Duncan, Riana. *That's an excellent suggestion, Miss Triggs. Perhaps one of the men here would like to make it*, 1988. Cartoon showing a sexist boardroom. Modern Punch Cartoons, London. https://punch.photoshelter.com/image/I0000BaPhg4sVCD4.

Eilperin, Juliet. "White House Women Want to be in the Room Where It Happens." *Washington Post*. September 13, 2016. https://www.washingtonpost.com/news/powerpost/wp/2016/09/13/white-house-women-are-now-in-the-room-where-it-happens/.

Engel, Beverly. "How Being Too Nice Can Be Dangerous for Women." *Psychology Today*. August 8, 2019. https://www.psychologytoday.com/us/blog/the-compassion-chronicles/201908/how-being-too-nice-can-be-dangerous-women.

Erasmus, Estelle. "Why Author Marissa Orr Leaned Out Instead of In, and How You Can Too." *Forbes*. May 26, 2019. https://www.forbes.com/sites/estelleerasmus/2019/05/26/why-author-marissa-orr-leaned-out-instead-of-in-and-how-you-can-too/?sh=bd04422e80e2.

Evans, Tom. "Ethnicity Pay Gaps in Great Britain: 2018." Earnings and Working Hours. Office for National Statistics. Posted July 9, 2019. https://www.ons.gov.uk/employmentandlabourmarket/peopleinwork/earningsandworkinghours/articles/ethnicitypaygapsingreatbritain/2018.

Exley, Christina L., and Judd B. Kessler. "The Gender Gap in Self-Promotion." National Bureau of Economic Research. Published October 2019. Revised May 2021. https://www.doi.org/10.3386/w26345.

Fashion United. "Redefining Plus Size – Dressing the 'Average' Woman in Europe." News. Business. Posted January 14, 2020. https://fashionunited.uk/news/business/redefining-plus-size-dressing-the-average-woman-in-europe/2020011447030.

Ferris, W. F., and N. J. Crowther. "Once Fat Was Fat and That Was That: Our Changing Perspectives on Adipose Tissue." *Cardiovascular Journal of Africa* 22, no. 3 (June 2011): 147–54. https://doi.org/10.5830/cvja-2010-083.

Fox, Michelle. "The 'Motherhood Penalty' Is Real, and It Costs Women $16,000 a Year in Lost Wages." Closing the Gap. CNBC. Updated March 25, 2019. https://www.cnbc.com/2019/03/25/the-motherhood-penalty-costs-women-16000-a-year-in-lost-wages.html.

Frankiewicz, Becky. "5 Ways We Lack Gender Balance in the Workplace." Davos 2020. World Economic Forum. Posted January 30, 2020. https://www.weforum.org/agenda/2020/01/5-ways-companies-can-progress-more-women-into-leadership-roles/.

Freud, Sigmund. *Three Essays on the Theory of Sexuality: The 1905 Edition*. Brooklyn: Verso, 2017.

Gardner, Amanda. "Many Obese Americans Struggle With Stigma, Discrimination, Poll Finds." Health Day. Posted August 23, 2012. https://consumer.healthday.com/vitamins-and-nutrition-information-27/obesity-health-news-505/many-obese-americans-struggle-with-stigma-discrimination-poll-finds-667697.html.

Germano, Maggie. "Women are Working More Than Ever, but They Still Take on Most Household Responsibilities." *Forbes*. Posted March 27, 2019. https://www.forbes.com/sites/maggiegermano/2019/03/27/women-are-working-more-than-ever-but-they-still-take-on-most-household-responsibilities/?sh=46a83bb752e9.

GOOP Podcast. "Gwyneth x Oprah: Power, Perception & Soul Purpose." March 8, 2018. Produced by Gwyneth Paltrow along with Boll & Branch, podcast, 1:16:01. https://goop.com/the-goop-podcast/gwyneth-x-oprah-power-perception-soul-purpose/.

Gordon, Aubrey. "'Fat' Isn't a Bad Word—It's Just the Way I Describe My Body." Opinion. Self. Posted May 28, 2021. https://www.self.com/story/fat-isnt-bad-word.

Grimshaw, Damian, and Jill Rubery. "The Motherhood Pay Gap: A Review of the Issues, Theory, and International Evidence." European Institute for Gender Equality. International Labour Office. https://eige.europa.eu/resources/wcms_371804.pdf.

Grose, Jessica. "Why Dads Don't Take Parental Leave." *New York Times*. February 19, 2020. https://www.nytimes.com/2020/02/19/parenting/why-dads-dont-take-parental-leave.html.

Hannon, Kerry. "The No.1 Way Women Can Succeed at Work." *Forbes*. April 24, 2014. https://www.forbes.com/sites/nextavenue/2014/04/24/the-no-1-way-women-can-succeed-more-at-work/?sh=3db0db49b17c.

Harts, Minda. *The Memo: What Women of Color Need to Know to Secure a Seat at the Table*. New York City: Seal Press, 2019.

Havard, Tirion. "Domestic Abuse and Covid-19: A Year into the Pandemic." Insight. House of Commons Library. Posted May 11, 2021. https://commonslibrary.parliament.uk/domestic-abuse-and-covid-19-a-year-into-the-pandemic/.

Higginbotham, Evelyn Brooks. *Righteous Discontent: The Women's Movement in the Black Baptist Church*, 1880–1920. Cambridge: Harvard University Press, 1993.

Hildreth, Cade. "Gender Spectrum: A Scientist Explains Why Gender Isn't Binary." *Blog*. Cade Hildreth. February 5, 2022. https://cadehildreth.com/gender-spectrum/.

Holmes, Connor. "What Employers Can Do to Support Women's Mental Health." Mental Health. Spring Health. Posted March 22, 2021. https://www.springhealth.com/what-employers-can-do-to-support-womens-mental-health/.

Holpuch, Amanda. "The 'Shecession': Why Economic Crisis is affecting Women More Than Men." *Guardian*. August 4, 2020. https://www.theguardian.com/business/2020/aug/04/shecession-coronavirus-pandemic-economic-fallout-women.

Hughes, Bettany. "Why Were Women Written Out of History? An Interview with Bethany Hughes." *History Uncovered* (blog). English Heritage. Posted February 29, 2016. https://blog.english-heritage.org.uk/women-written-history-interview-bettany-hughes/.

Hymas, Charles. "Women Face 'Motherhood Penalty' of Up to 45 Percent Lower Earnings." *Telegraph*. July 27, 2019, 9:00 p.m. GMT. https://www.telegraph.co.uk/news/2021/07/27/women-face-motherhood-penalty-45-per-cent-lower-earnings/.

Jeffreys, Branwen. "Do Children in Two-Parent Families Do Better?" BBC. February 5, 2019. https://www.bbc.co.uk/news/education-47057787.

Jerald, Casey. "Embrace Your Raw, Strange Magic." Filmed December 2018. TED Salon Belonging video, 16:55. https://www.ted.com/talks/casey_gerald_embrace_your_raw_strange_magic?language=en.

Kang, Sonia K., Katherine A. DeCelles, András Tilcsik, and Sora Jun. "Whitened Résumés: Race and Self-Presentation in the Labor Market." *Administrative Science Quarterly* 61, no. 3 March 2016): 469–502, https://doi.org/10.1177/0001839216639577.

Kashtan, Miki. "Why Patriarchy Is Not About Men." *Psychology Today.* August 4, 2017. https://www.psychologytoday.com/gb/blog/acquired-spontaneity/201708/why-patriarchy-is-not-about-men.

Kay, Katty, and Claire Shipman. "The Confidence Gap." *Atlantic.* May 2014. https://www.theatlantic.com/magazine/archive/2014/05/the-confidence-gap/359815/.

Kilpi, Fanny, Hanna Konttinen, Karri Silventoinen, and Pekka Martikainen. "Living Arrangements as Determinants of Myocardial Infarction Incidence and Survival: A Prospective Register Study of Over 300,000 Finnish Men and Women." *Social Science and Medicine* 133, (May 2015): 93–100. https://doi.org/10.1016/j.socscimed.2015.03.054.

King, Don Roy, dir. *Saturday Night Live.* Season 33, episode 5, "Weekend Update." Written by Seth Meyers, Paula Pell, and Andrew Steele. Featuring Tina Fey, Carrie Underwood, Amber Lee Ettinger, Steve Martin, Mike Huckabee, Don Pardo, and Casey Wilson. Aired February 23, 2008, on NBC. https://www.nbc.com/saturday-night-live/video/february-23-tina-fey/4017406.

Lee, Sun Y., Selin Kesebir, and Madan M. Pillutla. "Gender Differences in Response to Competition with Same-Gender Coworkers: A Relational Perspective." *Journal of Personality and Social Psychology* 110, no. 6 (2016): 869–86. https://doi.org/10.1037/pspi0000051.

Lerner, Gerda. *The Creation of the Patriarchy.* New York City: Oxford University Press, 1987.

Levine, Stuart R. and Thought Leaders. "Diversity Confirmed To Boost Innovation And Financial Results." *Forbes.* Posted January 15, 2020. https://www.forbes.com/sites/forbesinsights/2020/01/15/diversity-confirmed-to-boost-innovation-and-financial-results/?sh=1a9abdc4a6a5.

Lewis, Ruth, and Cicely Marston. "Oral Sex, Young People, and Gendered Narratives of Reciprocity." *Journal of Sex Research* 53, no. 7 (September 2016): 776–87. https://doi.org/10.1080/00224499.2015.1117564.

Lind, D. Scott, Stelios Rekkas, V. Bui, T. Lam, E. Beierle, and E. M. Copeland III. "Competency-Based Student Self-Assessment on a Surgery Rotation." *Journal of Surgical Research* 105, no. 1 (June 2002): 31–44. https://doi.org/10.1006/jsre.2002.6442.

Lipman, Joanne. "Women Are Still Not Asking for Pay Rises. Here's Why." Book Club. World Economic Forum. Posted April 12, 2018. https://www.weforum.org/agenda/2018/04/women-are-still-not-asking-for-pay-rises-here-s-why/.

Lorenzo, Rocío, Nicole Voigt, Miki Tsusaka, and Katie Abouzahr. "How Diverse Leadership Teams Boost Innovation." Boston Consulting Group. Posted January 23, 2018. https://www.bcg.com/publications/2018/how-diverse-leadership-teams-boost-innovation.

Lupton, Deborah. "What Does Fat Discrimination Look Like?" *Conversation.* January 2, 2013. https://theconversation.com/what-does-fat-discrimination-look-like-10247.

Macharia, Sarah, and Marcus Burke. "Just 24% of News Sources Are Women. Here's Why That's a Problem." World Economic Forum. Posted March 2, 2020. https://www.weforum.org/agenda/2020/03/women-representation-in-media/.

Majia, Zameena. "How to Combat 'Hepeating' at Work, According to a Harvard Professor." CNBC. Updated October 11, 2017. https://www.cnbc.com/2017/10/11/how-to-combat-hepeating-at-work-according-to-a-harvard-professor.html.

Martin, Sean R. "Research: Men Get Credit for Voicing Ideas, but Not Problems. Women Don't Get Credit for Either." *Harvard Business Review.* November 2, 2017. https://hbr.org/2017/11/research-men-get-credit-for-voicing-ideas-but-not-problems-women-dont-get-credit-for-either.

Mathews, Jane. "Katie Hopkins Says Women Should Sleep with Their Bosses to Get Ahead." *Daily Express.* July 24, 2014, 10:31 a.m. https://www.express.co.uk/news/uk/491280/Katie-Hopkins-says-women-should-sleep-with-their-bosses-to-get-ahead.

McIntosh, Peggy. *White Privilege and Male Privilege: A Personal Account of Coming to See Correspondences Through Work in Women's Studies.* 1988. https://www.collegeart.org/pdf/diversity/white-privilege-and-male-privilege.pdf.

Mercado, Darla. "Here's the Ken Fisher Audio that Inflamed Executives at a Financial Conference." Personal Finance. CNBC. Posted October 11, 2019.

Miller, Claire Cain, Kevin Quealy, and Margot Sanger-Katz. "The Top Jobs Where Women Are Outnumbered by Men Named John." *New York Times.* April 24, 2018. https://www.nytimes.com/interactive/2018/04/24/upshot/women-and-men-named-john.html.

Mohr, Tara Sophia. "Why Women Don't Apply for Jobs Unless They're 100% Qualified." *Harvard Business Review.* August 25, 2014. https://hbr.org/2014/08/why-women-dont-apply-for-jobs-unless-theyre-100-qualified.

Mooney, Attracta. "Female Hedge Funds Outperform Those Run by Men." *Financial Times*. September 16, 2017. https://www.ft.com/content/8bffa2c4-99f3-11e7-a652-cde3f882dd7b.

Narsaria, Anupriya. "Why Are Boys Not Allowed to Play with Dolls?" Science ABC. Updated January 22, 2022. https://www.scienceabc.com/social-science/why-are-boys-not-allowed-to-play-with-dolls.html.

O'Connor, Becky. "Rise of the female breadwinner: Woman earns the most in one-in-four households." Royal London. Posted May 27, 2020. https://www.royallondon.com/media/press-releases/archive/female-breadwinner-rise/.

Olfman, Sharna. "Gender, Patriarchy, and Women's Mental Health: Psychoanalytic Perspectives." *Journal of the American Academy of Psychoanalysis* 22, no. 2 (June 1994): 259–71. https://doi.org/10.1521/jaap.1.1994.22.2.259.

Orr, Marissa. *Lean Out: The Truth about Women, Power, and the Workplace*. Nashville: HarperCollins Leadership, 2019.

Parker, Kim. "Women in Majority-Male Workplaces Report Higher Rates of Gender Discrimination." Gender Equality and Discrimination. Pew Research Center. Posted March 7, 2018. https://www.pewresearch.org/fact-tank/2018/03/07/women-in-majority-male-workplaces-report-higher-rates-of-gender-discrimination/.

Payne, Christopher S. "Leisure Time in the UK." Satellite Accounts. Office for National Statistics. Posted October 24, 2017. https://www.ons.gov.uk/economy/nationalaccounts/satelliteaccounts/articles/leisuretimeintheuk/2015.

Petter, Olivia. "Being a Mother is Equivalent to 2.5 Full-Time Jobs, Survey Finds." *Independent* (March 2018). https://www.independent.co.uk/life-style/health-and-families/mother-equivalent-2-jobs-full-time-childcare-98-hours-work-mum-survey-a8258676.html.

——. "What is Hepeating?" *Independent*. November 29, 2017. https://www.independent.co.uk/life-style/hepeating-what-woman-ignore-men-idea-repeat-sexism-misogynist-a8080601.html.

Poehler, Amy. *Yes Please*. New York: HarperCollins, 2014.

Powell, Robyn. "How to Include Disabled Women in the Fight for Equal Pay." News. Bustle. Posted April 10, 2018. https://www.bustle.com/p/disabled-womens-equal-pay-struggles-often-go-unheard-but-you-can-help-include-them-8730123#:~:text=Women%20with%20disabilities%20face%20a%20striking%20wage%20gap%2C68%20cents%20for%20every%20dollar%20non-disabled%20people%20earned.

Puhl, Rebecca, and Kelly D. Brownell. "Bias, Discrimination, and Obesity." *Wiley Obesity Reviews* 12, no. 9 (September 2012): 788–805. https://doi.org/10.1038/oby.2001.108.

Querry, Kimberly. "Oklahoma City Apartment Complex Catches Fire, 5 Units Damaged; Sweet Brown Explains." Oklahoma News 4: KFOR-TV. Updated April 9, 2012, 11:13 a.m. CDT. https://kfor.com/news/okc-apartment-complex-catches-fire-5-units-damaged/.

Quinn, Margaret M., and Peter M. Smith. "Gender, Work, and Health." *Annals of Work Exposures and Health* 62, no. 4 (May 2018): 389–92. https://doi.org/10.1093/annweh/wxy019.

Rabbitt, Meghan. "How to Address Mental Health In the Workplace." *Woman's Day*. January 21, 2020. https://www.womansday.com/life/a30501058/mental-health-in-the-workplace/.

Randstad. *Women in Construction: Building Pace Post-Brexit.* Lufton, UK: Randstad, 2020. https://email.randstad.co.uk/download-women-in-construction.

Reid, Erin. "Embracing, Passing, Revealing, and the Ideal Worker Image: How People Navigate Expected and Experienced Professional Identities." *Organization Science* 26, no. 4 (July–August 2015): 941–1261. https://doi.org/10.1287/orsc.2015.0975.

Rigoglioso, Marguerite. "Researchers: How Women Can Succeed in the Workplace." Management. Stanford Graduate School of Business. Posted March 1, 2011. https://www.gsb.stanford.edu/insights/researchers-how-women-can-succeed-workplace.

Ritchie, Hannah, Max Roser, and Esteban Ortiz-Spinosa. "Suicide by Gender." *Our World in Data* (2015). https://ourworldindata.org/suicide#suicide-by-gender.

Russo, Gianluca. "How Fatphobia Has Cemented Itself in the American Workplace." Beauty. Nylon. Posted November 30, 2020. https://www.nylon.com/beauty/how-fatphobia-has-cemented-itself-in-the-american-workplace.

Sandstrom, Aleksandra. "Women Relatively Rare in Top Positions of Religious Leadership." Pew Research Center. Posted March 2, 2016. https://www.pewresearch.org/fact-tank/2016/03/02/women-relatively-rare-in-top-positions-of-religious-leadership/.

Sanghani, Radhika. "Sisterhood Ceiling: Are Women Holding Each Other Back in the Workplace?" *Telegraph*. April 15, 2016. https://www.telegraph.co.uk/women/work/sisterhood-ceiling-are-women-really-holding-each-other-back-in-t/.

Segel, Liz Hilton, and Kana Enomoto. "5 Ways Employers Can Support Women's Mental Health." *Harvard Business Review*. June 11, 2021. https://hbr.org/2021/06/5-ways-employers-can-support-womens-mental-health.

Shaw, Bart, Loic Menzies, Eleanor Bernardes, Sam Baars, Philip Nye, and Rebecca Allen. "Ethnicity, Gender and Social Mobility." Social Mobility Commission. Published 2016. https://assets.publishing.service.gov.uk/government/uploads/system/uploads/attachment_data/file/579988/Ethnicity_gender_and_social_mobility.pdf.

Shinall, Jennifer Bennett. "Occupational Characteristics and the Obesity Wage Penalty." SSRN. Revised April 30, 2016. https://papers.ssrn.com/sol3/papers.cfm?abstract_id=2379575.

Singer, Maya. "Why the Fashion World Needs to Commit to an 18+ Modeling Standard." *Vogue*. August 16, 2018. https://www.vogue.com/article/why-fashion-needs-to-commit-to-age-appropiate-modeling-standard-vogue-september-2018.

Sky, Jennifer. "Does Fashion Week Exploit Teen Models?" *Daily Beast*. July 12, 2017, 6:27p.m. ET. https://www.thedailybeast.com/does-fashion-week-exploit-teen-models.

Smith, Ella L. J. Edmondson, and Stella M. Nkomo. *Our Separate Ways: Black and White Women and the Struggle for Professional Identity* (Boston: Harvard Business School Press, 2001).

Smith, Hayley. "'Just Living with Pain': Women's Healthcare Waylaid by COVID-19 Pandemic." *Los Angeles Times*. Updated February 22, 2021, 7:29 a.m. PT. https://www.latimes.com/california/story/2021-02-22/covid-19-pandemic-womens-wellness-effects.

Staglin, Garen. "Employers Must Rise to the Challenge of Supporting Women in the Workplace." *Forbes*. March 10, 2021. https://www.forbes.com/sites/onemind/2021/03/10/employers-must-rise-to-the-challenge-of-supporting-women-in-the-workplace/?sh=2c5e56f11496.

Stuppy, Anika. "Why Power And Testosterone Are A Seriously Dangerous Mix." *Forbes*. Posted July 25, 2018. https://www.forbes.com/sites/rsmdiscovery/2018/07/25/why-power-and-testosterone-are-a-seriously-dangerous-mix/?sh=7108ca595d98.

Sud, Amit, Bethany Torr, Michael E. Jones, John Broggio, Stephen Scott, Chey Loveday, Alice Gerrett, Firza Gronthoud, David L. Nicol, Shaman Jhanji, Stephen A. Boyce, Matthew Williams, Elio Riboli, David C. Muller, Emma Kipps, James Larkin, Neal Navani, Charles Swanton, Georgios Lyratzopoulos, Ethna McFerran, and Mark Lawler. "Effect of Delays in the 2-Week-Wait Cancer Referral Pathway During the COVID-19 Pandemic on Cancer Survival in the UK: A Modelling Study." *Lancet Oncology* 21, no. 8 (August 2020): 1035–44. https://doi.org/10.1016/S1470-2045(20)30392-2.

Sutin, Angelina R., Yannick Stephan, and Antonio Terracciano. "Weight Discrimination and Risk of Mortality." *Psychological Science* 26, no. 11 (September 2015): 1803–11. https://doi.org/10.1177/0956797615601103.

Taylor, Jon. "Less than a Third of Eligible Men Take Paternity Leave." Latest. EMW LLP. July 8, 2019. https://www.emwllp.com/latest/less-than-a-third-of-men-take-paternity-leave/.

Taylor, S. E., L. C. Klein, B. P. Lewis, T. L. Gruenewald, R. A. Gurung, and J. A. Updegraff. "Biobehavioral Responses to Stress in Females: Tend-and-Befriend, Not Fight-or-Flight." *Psychological Review* 107, no. 3 (July 2000): 411–29. https://doi.org/10.1037/0033-295x.107.3.411.

Tulshyan, Ruchika. "Women and Office Politics: Play the Game or Lose." *Forbes*. November 20, 2013. https://www.forbes.com/sites/ruchikatulshyan/2013/11/20/women-and-office-politics-play-the-game-or-lose/?sh=14c145dfa8d2.

—— and Jodi-Ann Burey. "Stop Telling Women They Have Imposter Syndrome." *Harvard Business Review*. February 11, 2021. https://hbr.org/2021/02/stop-telling-women-they-have-imposter-syndrome.

UC San Diego Center on Gender Equity and Health. "Measuring #Me Too: A National Study on Sexual Harassment and Assault." Stop Street Harassment. April 2019. https://stopstreetharassment.org/wp-content/uploads/2012/08/2019-MeToo-National-Sexual-Harassment-and-Assault-Report.pdf.

Unwin, Lisa, and Deborah Khan. "Women, Play the Long Game." Organizations and People. Strategy + Business. Posted February 2, 2017. https://www.strategy-business.com/blog/Women-Play-the-Long-Game.

Usborne, Simon. "'It Was Seen as Weird': Why Are So Few Men Taking Shared Parental Leave?" *Guardian*. October 5, 2019. https://www.theguardian.com/lifeandstyle/2019/oct/05/shared-parental-leave-seen-as-weird-paternity-leave-in-decline.

Vaid-Menon, Alok. *Beyond the Gender Binary* (New York: Penguin Workshop, 2020). Washington, Zuhaira. and Laura M. Roberts. "Women of Color Get Less Support at Work. Here's How Managers Can Change That." *Harvard Business Review*. March 4, 2019. https://hbr.org/2019/03/women-of-color-get-less-support-at-work-heres-how-managers-can-change-that.

Weiss, Suzannah. "Women's Value Doesn't Just Lie in Pleasing Others." *Bustle*. August 15, 2016. https://www.bustle.com/articles/178718-6-ways-women-are-taught-to-please-other-people-why-they-dont-have-to.

Wellcome Trust. "Testosterone Makes Us Less Cooperative and More Egocentric." Science News. Science Daily. Posted January 31, 2012. www.sciencedaily.com/releases/2012/01/120131210259.htm.

Westwater, Hannah, Ella Glover, and Isabella McRae. "UK poverty: the facts, figures and effects." Social Justice. Big Issue. Posted March 24, 2022. https://www.bigissue.com/news/social-justice/uk-poverty-the-facts-figures-and-effects/.

Woetzel, Jonathan, Anu Madgavkar, Kweilin Ellingrud, Eric Labaye, Sandrine Devillard, Eric Kutcher, James Manyika, Richard Dobbs, and Mekala Krishnan. "The Power of Parity: How Advancing Women's Equality Can Add $12 Trillion to Global Growth." McKinsey & Company. September 2015. https://www.mckinsey.com/~/media/mckinsey/industries/public%20and%20social%20sector/our%20insights/how%20advancing%20womens%20equality%20can%20add%2012%20trillion%20to%20global%20growth/mgi%20power%20of%20parity_full%20report_september%202015.pdf.

Wolf, Naomi. *The Beauty Myth* (London: Chatto & Windus, 1990).

ACKNOWLEDGMENTS

Jenni would like to thank:

First and foremost, thank you to Lisa. Ik lief jou. Without you, none of this would be possible. You have been the best partner, confidante, and friend. Thank you for pushing us to finish this book and dare to dream that this could be our path towards a life of passion and purpose. Thank you for dragging me over the finish line when I was drowning in the darkest season of my life. To Alex, for holding down the fort and being cautiously optimistic while I tried to lasso the moon and shoehorn more hours in the day. To my sweet babies for believing in me and seeing a version of me that I will always try to live up to. Thank you to Debbie, Mark, Dima, and Nicky for always being the first to like our posts and validate our work. Thank you to everyone who ignored our work for showing us that we never needed you to succeed.

Lisa would like to thank:

Mark, Dima & Nicky – our most steadfast social media soldiers since the start. Charlie, for reading the roughs. Oscar, for helping me think about both sides of every argument, Amelie, for being naturally fierce & helping Dad understand what I was always going on about, and Isaac, who gives the best support hugs. Emma, for all the walks, laughter, and sisterly love. Justin, just because. Scott, for wanting to learn and (slowly) becoming a better feminist each day. Rufus, the reason I plant trees whose shade I will never sit under.

And Jenni, for making me believe that we were allowed to create & hold this space; the book, the podcast, all of it exists because of you. Ik lief jou.

Author Bio

JENNIFER AUDRIE has worked in both tech and finance for the better part of the last twenty years, working for a range of high profile corporations. She now uses her wide breadth of knowledge to educate start-ups and small businesses on foundational business practices and helps them gain traction in the market using evolving digital strategies. She was a Riggio Scholar at the New School where she earned her BA in liberal arts and lives in Charlotte, NC with her partner and three children. She is the co-host of the "Dear Patriarchy" podcast.

LISA LYNN has spent the last twenty years working in the finance and construction industries and has project managed countless landmark London build projects where she developed and supported women-fronted construction teams. She now works alongside Jennifer supporting entrepreneurs in developing bespoke business strategies to support long-term growth using a data-led approach. She holds a master's degree in project management and lives with her partner and son in Hertfordshire, England. She is the co-host of the "Dear Patriarchy" podcast.